W9-BUM-223

"Not in Front
of the Children . . ."

Also by Dr. Lawrence Balter

Who's in Control? Dr. Balter's Guide to Discipline
Without Combat

Dr. Balter's Child Sense

FOR CHILDREN
Sue Lee Starts School
A Funeral for Whiskers
Linda Saves the Day
The Wedding
What's the Matter with A.J.?
Sue Lee's New Neighborhood
A.J.'s Mom Gets a New Job
Alfred Goes to the Hospital

"Not in Front of the Children..."

How to Talk to Your Child About
Tough Family Matters

DR. LAWRENCE BALTER

with Peggy Jo Donahue

V I K I N G
A Skylight Press Book

VIKING
Published by the Penguin Group
Penguin Books USA Inc., 375 Hudson Street,
New York, New York 10014, U.S.A.
Penguin Books Ltd, 27 Wrights Lane,
London W8 5TZ, England
Penguin Books Australia Ltd, 10 Alcorn Avenue,
Toronto, Ontario, Canada M4V 3B2
Penguin Books (N.Z.) Ltd, 182–190 Wairau Road,
Auckland 10, New Zealand

Penguin Books Ltd, Registered Offices:
Harmondsworth, Middlesex, England

First published in 1993 by Viking Penguin,
a division of Penguin Books USA Inc.

10 9 8 7 6 5 4 3 2 1

Copyright © Lawrence Balter and Skylight Press, 1993
All rights reserved

Published by arrangement with
Skylight Press
166 East 56th Street
New York, NY 10022

LIBRARY OF CONGRESS CATALOGING-IN-PUBLICATION DATA
Balter, Lawrence.
    "Not in front of the children . . ." /
by Lawrence Balter with Peggy Jo Donahue.
    p. cm.
    "A Skylight Press book."
    ISBN 0-670-84110-2
    1. Parenting—Moral and ethical aspects. 2. Parent and child—
Moral and ethical aspects. 3. Communication in the family.
I. Donahue, Peggy Jo. II. Title.
HQ755.85.B34 1993
306.874—dc20   92-50400

Printed in the United States of America
Set in New Baskerville
Designed by Ann Gold

To truth-seekers everywhere, young and old.

And to Karen, forever.

   —L.B.

To my family, Bill, Sarah, and Billy,
who talk about their feelings honestly.

   —P.J.D.

Contents

"Not in Front
of the Children . . ."

1
The Myth of Family Secrets: How Much Should Our Children Really Know?

"**N**ot in front of the children." At one time or another almost every parent has uttered these words. Why? Because most of us have a deep and abiding interest in protecting our children from stresses they may be too young to handle. Whether the situation involves a heated argument between husband and wife, sobs of grief upon the death of a loved one, or even just a discussion about the straitened monthly budget, parents forever worry about the extent of emotional damage suffered by a child who has been forced to witness such a scene.

Yet anxiety-inducing events occur in all households, and while it's true that few young children are equipped on their own to cope with the worst of these, a great deal of harm can also be done by always keeping children in the dark.

Because of this dilemma, most loving and thoughtful parents would like to know what they can do to at least

lessen a child's fright and pain when she or he witnesses a
family crisis.

- "I can't stand it anymore," you shout at your husband as
  you bolt from the house late one evening at the end of
  another bitter quarrel. "I've got to get out of here!" You
  don't see your four-year-old daughter eavesdropping
  from the top of the stairs, and you are already out the
  door when she asks her father in a tiny voice, her lip
  quivering, "Is Mommy coming back?"
- It's just after midnight. The children have been asleep
  for hours. You and your spouse begin making love. You
  suddenly become aware of your three-year-old standing
  beside the bed. "Daddy," his expression seems to ask,
  "what are you doing to Mommy?"
- You are sitting at the kitchen table, your head in your
  hands. The monthly bills are spread out before you.
  You've been out of work for months; with half the family
  income cut off, savings are almost exhausted. "I don't
  know how we're going to pay our bills this month, let
  alone buy Christmas gifts," you say aloud to your wife, a
  note of panic in your voice. Your seven-year-old daughter
  is loading the dishwasher and listening to music—you
  think. Suddenly, she bursts into tears and runs from the
  room.

Such scenes are enough to leave any parent riddled with
guilt. Why couldn't I have controlled myself? What can I
possibly do now? Will my child ever forgive me? Will he
carry this moment with him forever?

Your children will often see or hear more than you intend them to see or hear, and, sometimes, more than they
should see and hear. This is an inevitable part of family

life, and at times just cannot be helped, even in the most careful families.

Still, it must be noted that young children often misinterpret those unintended and unexpected glimpses they are permitted into the adult world. Unsophisticated, egocentric, and literal, they will interpret all that they see and hear as commentary on themselves or as clues to what the future may hold for them. The four-year-old who saw her mother storm from the house wonders, "Is Mommy mad at me? Will she ever come back?" The three-year-old who observes his parents making love may assume it as an act of aggression and wonder who is mad and who was bad. The seven-year-old, listening to her father's idle muttering over money problems, takes literally the prospect of a Christmas with no presents and is crushed by it. Or she may take on some of the blame for her father's sadness, worrying that instead of buying candy with the dollar her grandmother gave her maybe she should have offered it to her father.

There are also the tensions over serious ongoing family matters that children sense rather than witness directly. Should they be told that Aunt Sarah has cancer and may die? Is it time to mention that Mom and I have been talking about separation? Should I explain that Daddy has a health problem that may be serious?

And, finally, there are those events in every family's history that aren't discussed with children. When should I tell them I was previously married? Should I mention that their aunt once had a baby even though she wasn't married, and explain what that means? How old should they be before I tell them that their grandfather had a mental illness and eventually committed suicide?

Of the more current issues subject to taboo, conventional wisdom says that sex, divorce, serious illness or death, money problems, and substance abuse are never to be discussed in front of the children, though in my years as a child psychologist, I've learned that while you may succeed in keeping children from learning the details of certain family problems, there are very few thorny issues about which you can keep them totally in the dark. No matter how young they are, or how vigilantly you try to shield them, children sense when something is amiss.

There is nothing extrasensory going on here. Even before they understood a word of what you were saying to them, your children learned how to read your facial expressions and body language, your tone of voice, maybe the abruptness of your movements, for clues as to how they were about to be treated. It should not be surprising, then, that they remain sensitive to much more than those few spoken words directed at them. From the other side of the closed door they hear whispers or voices raised in argument, and they react to what they hear. Their ears perk up as quickly as any adult's when an ordinary dinner-table conversation deteriorates into a competition in biting sarcasm. They study the frown on your face as you agonize over whether or not to buy an expensive gift. When they stumble upon adults embracing in the shower, they note the looks of embarrassment on both faces.

In my private practice, and on my radio and television programs, I have spoken with thousands of parents who found themselves at a loss to explain difficult or stressful events to their children. They walk away, full of regret, thinking: "I can't believe I did that," or "I can't believe she saw that," or "Maybe I shouldn't have discussed this with the children at all."

Even the most confident, relaxed parents have moments when they torture themselves over such issues. But I believe much of this worry and concern can be avoided if parents understand more clearly what is at risk for their children, and what, specifically, they can do to minimize these risks.

Tempering the Truth

Every parent's classic but unrealistic fear is that exposing a child to something that he or she is not yet ready for will damage the child for life. Parents need to develop ways to talk about subjects as touchy as sex, divorce, death, money and work problems, substance abuse, and arguing, and to do so without the overriding fear that a misstep will doom their child to a life of emotional pain. This book will help you talk with your children about these topics with some lessened apprehension. It will also discuss how best to handle those regrettable but often unavoidable moments that may indeed seriously disturb your child.

It will also treat the difficult question of when and how children should be told about family secrets, the kind you so often keep from children because they are past history and because no moment seems right for bringing them up. In treating this issue, *"Not in Front of the Children . . ."* will necessarily raise some very tough but fundamental questions: When it comes to our young children, is honesty always the best policy? How much should our children be told about the skeletons in the family closet, and how much should we hold back? At what age and in what setting are children ready for unsettling information about family members?

These are particularly daunting questions because they involve the concept of truthfulness as a basis of trust among family members. It hardly needs saying that if a growing child learns that his parents cannot be relied upon for straight answers to his important questions about his own family, both child and parent will pay a price down the road. But if a child is too young to understand all the important concerns in an issue, throwing the raw truth at him, and all of it, may do far more damage than good. Going into gory detail about homicides or illnesses among family members is clearly neither necessary nor helpful. There will also be areas other than those involving family secrets where prudence suggests we hold off imparting the full story to a young child. Complex ethical issues such as euthanasia and abortion, whether or not they involve close family members, are not appropriate fare for a young child.

Present-Day Family Secrets: Should They Be Kept?

All families have secrets, things that are kept from children and from the outside world. The reasons vary family to family and secret to secret. The family may be undergoing financial difficulties that if widely known might disturb relationships with friends, extended family, or even business or professional associates. Or perhaps it's marital strife. Possibly it's a life-threatening illness. We keep up a good front.

We may feel that our children do not need to know too much about these problems, not only because we don't want them sharing personal information with friends and teachers, but also because we don't want to burden them. Simultaneously, we recognize that though we can keep the details of the secret from the child, we are not likely going to be able to keep her from sensing that something is afoot when that something seems to be threatening one or both of her parents, and may therefore soon threaten the child herself.

How much you decide to tell a child about these matters depends upon a number of factors. First, you must consider your child's ability to comprehend what you will be telling her. Whatever you decide to share with a child should be offered at the child's level of understanding. Next, you have to time the revelation so that it does not come as a shock. It is probably best if sensitive information is shared in small increments over an extended period of time.

As important as it is that you not deprive your child of the opportunity to develop his or her own skill in making good judgments about new information, it is just as important that you not throw heavy doses of unfiltered information at a child with no regard for how it will be received. How can you tell when you are at a point where holding back information can cause problems as serious as those you are trying to avert, where it risks that precious trust between you and your child? Your own comfort level must also be considered. Your own anxiety about a subject may lead you to present material in a way that will increase the child's apprehension that important information is being withheld. Once you decide to open the subject, you must be prepared to answer some very personal questions if they are asked, and to offer support if the child reacts emotionally to what you have said.

This book will offer guidelines on how much, and at what rate parents should tell children about touchy issues. The idea is to provide them, in doses so measured that the children are not unnecessarily disquieted, with enough information to teach them how to handle those stressful events that occur in every family. In doing so, you'll be "inoculating" them, so that by the time they grow up they'll have learned by your teaching and your example that uncomfortable subjects and feelings are a part of life. A part that can and must be revealed and discussed.

Hiding Too Much

You will often find yourself walking a fine line between saying too much and too little. In my discussions with patients and the public, however, I have found that adults have strongly negative feelings about having had family secrets kept from them in their own childhoods, and about the lies told to keep them from learning those secrets. Though some remember being disturbed at being told more than they wanted to hear, more remember with anger or disappointment those times when they belatedly discovered some family secret about which they long had had some suspicion, but about which they had been systematically deceived. It may well be that parents who find it hard to be honest with their children had parents who were not honest with them, and the book will discuss this aspect of the problem.

Here the some of the more common errors parents make:

• *Assuming your child is oblivious to the emotional undercurrents around the house.* Chances are she isn't. She may have heard whispered conversations. Unfamiliar people may have been dropping by. Perhaps you are away more. It is tempting to assume that because your child has said nothing, she has noticed nothing, but this abandons the child to her worst fears, those she has the most difficulty raising with you, and forces her to fashion her own explanations for the events she senses swirling around her. These fantasies can be—

and often are—far more disturbing than the reality you have been trying to spare her.

Besides all this, just the fact of being excluded can be unsettling for children, threatening as it does the special relationship between parent and child. Even good secrets, such as the contents of a wrapped gift, are very difficult for children to tolerate.

• *Saying nothing, but revealing anxiety through nonverbal cues.* If you are in the middle of a family crisis, even though you try to maintain the appearance of normality and manage to avoid all the whispering and other household disruptions that crises often bring, you may still be giving away the truth in other ways. Though you may not be aware that you do so, you convey your anxiety through your body language and other nonverbal means of communication. The rolling of eyes, the heaving sigh, the downward turn of your mouth, the knitting of brows, the fidgety fingers, or the distracted conversations you have with your child— all tell him that something is wrong. Even if he doesn't interpret all these signals correctly, he will know that something is amiss.

• *Insisting that nothing is wrong even after your child has asked you what's going on.* Quite clearly, this risks breaching the parent-child trust. In addition, since in this case your child has already sensed that all is not well, your denial will cause him to doubt his own intuition. When you say nothing is wrong, especially if there is an edge to your voice as you say it, you impart a belief that certain uncomfortable feelings or thoughts are not to be expressed. Children raised this way often begin to close down their natural inclination to talk about their feelings to others. They may also block those uncomfortable thoughts from their own minds and never learn to recognize and to deal with their own emotions in a forthright manner.

Revealing Too Much

While situations in which children are not told enough can cause confusion and upset, there are also occasions—and I'll cite some in the chapters to come—when parents reveal too much.

Many children engage in self-blame. Children forced to grapple with too many complex adult concerns can easily come to believe that they are the cause of these overwhelming problems. "If only I didn't ask for so many toys, Mommy and Daddy wouldn't fight so much," or, "If I could just be a good boy, Daddy would come to see me more often than he has since the divorce."

Under the weight of such pressures, some children regress. Alice, a young mother of two, consulted me about her eight-year-old son, Fred, who had become a behavior problem in school and had begun wetting the bed again. Recently divorced, Alice admitted that she relied heavily on Fred, confiding in him about her problems with his father and her money worries. She also called upon him to help care for his three-year-old brother. Too young to deal with these grown-up issues and responsibilities, yet unable to express his distress to his mother, Fred began regressing in an unconscious attempt to regain the old security of his lost childhood.

Another reaction of an overburdened child is denial. When a child is made privy to more than she can handle, she may cope by believing it to be untrue. Some children treat traumatic events as if those events were part of a dream or fantasy.

Dealing with Those "Skeletons in the Closet"

Not only do we hide day-to-day stresses, we also hide bigger family secrets, sometimes for decades. But if children learn while young—or even after they have become adults—that such secrets were kept from them, they often feel confused and betrayed. Why was the information kept from them? Aren't they part of the inner circle of the family entitled to know such things? What else do the other members of the family know that they don't? Aren't they respected enough to know the true history of the family?

Have you ever had the experience of learning about an important family secret years after the events took place? Uncle Ed may have been in prison, for example. Cousin Mary was adopted. Aunt Sophie was an alcoholic. How did you feel when you finally learned the truth?

As a young woman, Pam inadvertently learned that her mother's mother had been married before, a fact no one had ever told her. When she learned about it in her late teen years, she felt deceived. Why couldn't she have been told about it sooner? Was there something more to the story that she still hadn't been told? Her thoughts ran to all sorts of lurid possibilities. Was her grandmother's first husband a criminal whose record could cause the granddaughter embarrassment if her friends ever learned of it? She wondered what had happened to the man. She questioned whether there were children from that marriage, which would have meant that her mother had half siblings, and Pam had cousins she had never met. What could be so awful that she could not have been told? In Pam's case, it turned out not to be a case of trying to shield the family from the stigma of divorce. The man had been killed in the war, her mother explained to her. Now Pam was incredulous. What was so bad about Grandma having been widowed by war that the fact had to be kept secret from Pam for so many years? There has to be more to the story, she continues to believe.

You can spare children such vivid imaginings if you allow them over time to have all important information about their own family's history. In the chapters to come, I'll suggest how and when to do so.

Some family secrets concern the child too directly to be kept from the child for very long. A little girl who does not know she had an older sister who died is one example. A child who is not told that he's adopted is another. If a child stumbles across this kind of information about a subject so close to the child's image of herself, the discovery may shock her developing sense of reality, distorting or even damaging her perception of herself and of the truth.

Parents should not assume that secrets are safe from accidental discovery simply because the events occurred before the child's time. Children are endlessly rummaging through drawers and closets and into other hidden-away places, and eventually will almost certainly come across some bit of information that forces them to consider the possibility that some secret is being kept from them. One child I knew first found out that she had had an older brother who died when she was rooting through her mother's drawers one day and found some baby clothes and photographs with someone else's name on them.

Why do parents try to keep old secrets from their children? The first reason, of course, is that the secrets often involve painful memories, such as the remembrance of a relative who had a substance-abuse problem or a mental illness. Giving children the full facts about such problems forces the parent to relive the pain. Other secrets are embarrassing, and some may be difficult to communicate to young children in a way that will not cause them to doubt their own security. For instance, how do you tell your children that you were previously married? There are ways to reveal such difficult pieces of your history, and I will try within the pages of this book to help you find relatively safe and comfortable ways to convey to your own children accurate and age-appropriate information about the past.

Your Child's View

By revealing the sometimes enigmatic inner workings of a child's mind, this book will also help you understand how your children interpret what they see in the world around them, especially what grown-ups say and do. It will make you aware of the many ways you communicate to your children your fears and anxieties, your optimism or pessimism about the family's future, and of the many other mixed and garbled messages you send them without intending to do so. And it will teach you how to guide your children with insight, empathy, and purpose.

Chapter 3, "Through the Eyes of Children," will explore what researchers know about how children think. It will explain the different ways children at different developmental stages—in particular the toddler, preschooler, and young school-age child—are likely to interpret the realities of the adult world. Most parents will be surprised by the extent to which children twist little things they see and hear. Take an all-too-common situation, a couple arguing over the dinner table. When he sees and hears his parents' increasing anger, the two-year-old may fear that the harsh words are directed at him, and start to cry. His five-year-old sister may react with anxiety about her future security (Are my parents going to yell at me next? Are they going to leave me?). And their eight-year-old brother may slink away in mortification, sure the whole world now knows his parents don't get along.

This same chapter will also help you learn how your child's temperament can affect his vulnerability to future stresses. For instance, is your child the type who can be devastated by garden-variety bickering, or is he so resilient that he can survive even the dreadful fallout from divorce relatively unscathed? The answers to those questions will help guide you in tailoring to your own child's needs the information you choose to reveal at each stage of his childhood.

How Your Past Operates

Chapter 2, "The Parents' Perspective," explains how your own upbringing inevitably affects the way you choose to reveal family values to your children. How do you feel about money? Were you raised in a household where family income was strictly hush-hush? Or one in which money was talked about all the time? Was the weekly paycheck used as a cudgel in the power struggle between your parents? How about sex? Was it discussed openly and naturally—or whispered about with stammers and blushes?

"Not in Front of the Children . . ." will help you reach back into your past to enable you to understand why you may be uncomfortable talking about certain issues with your own children. It will also explain how your discomfort with certain subjects can send inconsistent or ambiguous messages to your children.

It will also help you understand how day-to-day dealings

with your children can trigger once-forgotten memories of your own childhood and your own parents, causing you to communicate with your kids in the same old way. As you become more aware of all those hidden feelings, conflicts, and prejudices that you bring to every family situation, you may be better able to understand your own behavior in relation to your children, and why you tend to deal with them as you do. What's more, you will be helped in understanding how your children are likely to interpret what you say and do.

How This Book Will Help You

The aim of *"Not in Front of the Children . . ."* is to aid you in your attempts to help your children understand adult situations that have an impact on their lives. Various chapters focus on subjects such as arguing, sex and nudity, divorce, illness and death, money, substance abuse, and talking about your children in front of them. Beginning with Chapter 4, each topic will have three clearly defined components:

• THE CHILD'S-EYE VIEW will explain how children at different developmental stages interpret what they see and hear and understand about the topic at hand. Information is provided for children in each of three age groups: Toddler (eighteen months to three years), Preschooler (three to five years), and Young School-Age Child (six to eight years).

• MISSTEPS PARENTS MAKE will alert you to those common errors parents make that contribute to a child's confusion.

• NEW MOVES will provide the words and strategies for helping young children of different stages of development come to grips with bewildering events or sophisticated issues.

Parents are faced daily with many difficult decisions regarding their children. Which day-care center should they be sent to, and later, which school? Which foods are best for them, and which toys? How do we best stimulate our children's intellectual capabilities? What's the best way to discipline them when discipline is needed?

But just as we wish to protect our children from physical harm and to give them the best education, we also agonize over their psychological health. It is my hope that with the help of this book you will be able to develop the knowledge and skills to communicate vital information to your children about delicate and often daunting subjects, and to do so effectively, clearly, and in ways that reduce the risk of psychological harm.

2
The Parents' Perspective

Whether you find yourself speaking openly on certain tough subjects and encouraging your child's questions, or cutting off all discussion and discouraging further questions, you must face that the way you have chosen to respond has been strongly influenced by how comfortable you are with the subjects your child is raising. It is therefore wise that you spend some time thinking about your own attitudes in certain difficult areas before you consider how to handle your children's questions in these areas.

The first task is to understand where your attitudes and feelings come from. Your own childhood and later experiences have exerted powerful influences on the attitudes you now hold, and contribute far more to the response you make to your child than the way he posed the question or the moment he chose to pose it. There may also be present tensions that are playing a role; your current situation can have an enormous effect on your readiness to hear your child on difficult matters. And when present pressures come together with a memory of how your parents handled similar situations, the way you deal with your kids becomes a complex mixture of past and present influences.

Sam is having serious financial problems, but finds himself utterly incapable of responding to his children's questions about the family's changed circumstances. His fears and the immediate pressure he's now under contribute greatly to his inability to respond to his children's understandable questions about what's going on. But he also remembers his own father, who throughout Sam's childhood always seemed to be having job and money troubles, and who regularly terrorized the family with dire warnings about "going broke." Sam cannot help wondering whether his inability to talk to his own children about his financial situation might be connected to an unwillingness to put himself, in the eyes of his own children, in the unattractive role in which he remembers his father.

An unhappy marriage is another example of a situation where present pressures can combine with the past in forging your response to your children. Mary, whose parents were divorced when she was a child, told me that she remembers being confused and devastated by her parents' failure to talk about the problem, leaving her to guess what was happening and how it would affect her. Now that she is going through her own divorce, she tells her children everything, including some adult matters that I believe her children are really too young to understand.

Of course, stresses in your present life need not be related to crises as serious as losing a job or getting a divorce. Today's parents can be under a great deal of pressure just trying to manage their lives and provide nurturing homes for their children. Long hours on the job, child-care responsibilities, and the meager amount of time left to build an adult relationship can all contribute to your inability to respond appropriately to sensitive topics raised by the kids. If you're already tired or stressed out, a school-age child's questions or accusations about your alcohol or cigarette use, a preschooler's sudden obsession with sex, a toddler's whiny clinging when you and your spouse fight, can push you over the edge. It goes without saying that an angry or impatient response in such a situation may create a sense of alarm in your child or suppress all future discussion, rather than quelling fear and encouraging communication.

Every parent will occasionally be inclined to react in such ways, but instead of silencing a question you are not prepared to answer just then, you might say, "I'm feeling very upset right now, but I will answer your questions later." If you have already blown up at your child, an apology and a simple explanation are in order. "I'm sorry that I screamed at you. Daddy and I were having a fight and I know that made you feel unhappy. But we've made up, so you don't have to worry. If you like, we can talk now."

It is important that you follow up when you feel yourself ready to give your child's concerns the time they need, for they will not go away until you help her understand what is provoking them. If you don't help her fashion explanations she can accept, you'll leave her with her own misinterpretations, which may frighten or confuse her.

Remembrance of Things Past

Your attitudes, manner, and tone of voice when dealing with your kids may be a legacy from your earliest memories of how your own parents handled the same issues. Every parent has had an experience similar to this: you're talking to—or yelling at—your child, and suddenly you say to yourself, in surprise, "I sound just like my father (or mother)." Such moments reveal the extent to which, often unwittingly, you have retained intact the model of parenting your own parents provided you. Your children catch you in a moment of short temper, and you find yourself assuming attitudes, using glares or even threatening gestures that can only have come from a long-buried memory of your own parent in a similar situation. Words stream out of your mouth, seemingly of their own volition, words that are not part of your everyday vocabulary. You are not at all sure why you've said what you've said, or why you've done something that you believe is entirely out of character for you. All you do know is that your actions are driven in these moments by emotions that run deep and strong.

As much as we try to be logical and rational, this child raising turns out to be a highly emotional business. Why else would so many parents find themselves oddly compelled to repeat parental mistakes they recall from a past that was painful and confusing? The answer has to do very much with the tremendous influence your parents had over you as a very young child. After all, your first and most powerful authority figures were your parents, and the things they told you constituted your blueprint for survival and success. Of course, your vision of your parents was from a vantage point that was actually quite distorted, for you had no basis for judging whether their words and actions conveyed real wisdom or were simply a flawed legacy from their own childhoods. But to any young child, parents seem to have the answer to every question and know how to behave in every situation. It is quite understandable, if not inevitable, then, that for a time children accept their own parents' example of parenthood as a proper model.

Think about how much your own children imitate you.

The way you walk, your speech patterns, your gestures are all thrown back at you—for better or for worse. One mother I know recalled explaining to her six-year-old daughter how the child might go about patching up a fight she had had with a friend. To the mother's amazement, the little girl went to the phone, called her friend, and repeated verbatim everything her mother had said!

Because most people enter parenthood having absorbed a great deal of the example set by their parents does not mean they will all react to all situations exactly as their parents might have, though the reactions of most people will have at least some relationship to that early and powerful exposure. In remembering the way your parents acted, and the pain it may have caused you, you may vow to act very differently with your own children. However—despite your best intentions—the more stress you are under, the more you will be pulled back to the model of parenting your own parents provided you. So you will have to exercise eternal vigilance in your dealings with your children, especially in those very moments when other pressures are distracting you.

Other parents have more pleasant memories of their childhood and so are more willing to allow them to define their role as parents. But be careful. You may catch yourself repeating mistakes your parents made simply because rejecting their example might force you to reappraise your generally favorable judgment of them as parents.

Or, to the contrary, you may be unable to face how truly unpleasant your childhood was and sense that going back over your parents' destructive ways of dealing with you, and how much misery they caused you, will force you to relive it all. A man I've known for years is an example of this last. He has repeatedly described for me how cruel and mean-spirited his own father was in disciplining him, though I have received the impression that he has never faced the pain this treatment caused him and that he's never gotten over it. Now that he has children of his own, he's convinced himself that his father's harsh treatment was the right way to go. "It was good for me. Toughened me up," he says now, and disciplines his own children the same way. Rather than face all the new anguish that he would have to endure in unearthing painful memories and seeing and accepting his father's wanton cruelty for what it was, he perpetuates the cycle by inflicting on his children the same treatment he suffered as a child.

You can also get into trouble when you vow to do things differently from the way your parents did them. An acquaintance of mine, who is terrified at the thought of being like his own mother, whom he remembers as being extremely overbearing in her dealings with her children, has trouble offering any kind of advice or help to his own son.

Aside from any unpleasant memories you are holding of your own treatment as a child, there are also feelings, experiences, and situations that you have buried—possibly because they were too painful to keep in your conscious memory—that nevertheless continue to exert a powerful influence on the way you treat your own children, simply because they played so important a role in your development. In no area of child raising will this be more true than in the way you talk with your children about the sensitive topics I'll cover in this book.

Unearthing the Past

Your inability to remember specific experiences from your childhood probably has a great deal to do with how young you were when the events occurred. If you were very young, you didn't have a great deal of language to attach to what you were experiencing. And you didn't have the logic or the ability to categorize or classify the experience, thus making it harder to store the memory so that you could easily retrieve it. When you add to this the mind's natural inclination to insulate from easy recall events that are painful and upsetting, you can see why so many of us repress so many childhood memories.

To jog your memory and get into the process of reviewing your own past, you may want to ask yourself the following questions about your own childhood, perhaps jotting down some notes on the memories each brings to mind. Write down the first thing that comes to mind, allowing yourself no more than ten or fifteen seconds to think about each question.

- What do you think was the worst mistake your (mother) (father) made in bringing you up?
- What was the most painful part of your home life?
- What did you like about the way your (mother) (father) talked to you?
- What did you dislike about the way your parents talked to you?
- Can you think of a scene you wish you hadn't witnessed?
- What embarrassed you the most about your family in front of your friends?
- Do you remember feeling responsible for a family crisis?
- Were you ever afraid that either of your parents would abandon you?
- What did you envy most about other people's home lives?

After you have gone through these questions, you might then think about the following questions, based on topics I will cover in later chapters:

- Was sex ignored when you were growing up? Was it spoken of with embarrassment? Were questions about sex answered openly, or were they brushed off? How did this make you feel? I know a man who has never forgotten the trauma of asking his father to explain about "girls," only to have his father brusquely reject the question and stalk away.
- Do you remember how your parents argued with each other? Were there screaming fights, and if so, did they frighten you? At the other extreme, were all bad feelings and open disagreements suppressed? Did you have the uneasy feeling that something was wrong between your parents, but not know exactly what it was?
- How about money matters? Was there hand-wringing and constant complaining about the shortage of money? Did you ever worry that your family would be out on the street?
- What about illness and death? When someone died, did people walk around talking in hushed tones or clam up when you or your siblings came into the room? Was the death or serious illness of someone close ever kept from you?
- If someone in your family abused drugs or alcohol, did either parent try to keep this information from you? Or were you encouraged to believe that it was normal to have a drunk parent? Did you ever feel as though you might have to take over? If you did, how did you feel about this prospect?
- If your parents were divorced, do you remember wishing

that they would reunite? Did you ever worry that your noncustodial parent would abandon you forever?

Don't be afraid to add your own questions to this brief exercise, and remember that the harder a question for you to ask yourself, the more relevant the answer is likely to be.

It's hard to face the mistakes your parents made in your own upbringing, and the negative and destructive impact these mistakes may have had on your own personality. But you owe it to your children to think through these issues. If you fail to do so, you will be unable to interrupt the destructive cycle and may find yourself passing on to your own children the very same kinds of pain you were dealt as a child.

Jane, a woman I treated, waged a long-simmering argument with her husband for spending so much time away from the family. She knew that resorting to sarcasm in front of the children wasn't the best way to express her anger, but she couldn't stop herself from throwing out barbs whenever her husband was on his way out the door. "Wave goodbye to Daddy, children," Jane would say sweetly. "He has a very important golf outing that's much more important than we are!" She knew from the confused looks on the faces of her six-year-old and eight-year-old that she was not doing the children any good, that such sarcasm was baffling and hurting them, but she didn't know how else to have it out with her husband.

I was immediately reminded of a story Jane had told me earlier about how her own mother always hung "bumbling husband" cartoons on the refrigerator, cartoons that portrayed husbands doing insensitive, hurtful things to their wives, like forgetting an anniversary or not noticing how nice they looked. Jane recalled that though many of her mother's friends expressed amusement at the cartoons, her father simply glared at them, saying nothing. She had always felt troubled by all this, because she found these public jokes at her father's expense cruel and unfair.

When I pointed this out to her, Jane was able to see the link between her mother's oblique attacks on her father and the sarcasm she used as a replacement for direct confrontation with her own husband. She felt embarrassed and humiliated. "Gee, I'm such a fool. How could I have not realized I was doing the same thing? It's so obvious." But it isn't so obvious, I told her. We often put on blinders to protect ourselves from painful connections to our past.

It's never too late to correct a pattern, however, and Jane resolved to begin talking more directly to her husband about her feelings. Once she opened up these more direct avenues of communication, she no longer felt the need to use her kids as a captive audience for her sarcastic gibes at her husband.

Sarah has bitter memories of her father endlessly berating her mother. Her parents' arguments were not really arguments but monologues in which her father ranted on and on and her mother kept her silence, apparently so as not to further disturb the household. But Sarah remembers being badly shaken by the scenes. Despite her memory of the fear and pain this caused her as a child, she is repeating the pattern in her own marriage. This time around, however, she's the ranter, while her husband attempts to keep the peace. Her children are left to look on in fear, in the very same role she played many years ago.

Here is a case where a mother remembers a destructive pattern in her own parents' behavior in front of the kids, but has not yet seen a link between this behavior and her own. So she is repeating the pattern, taking for herself the active role, perhaps in response to having been forced as a child to be so passive a participant to the ugly tableau.

How Parents Can Break the Cycle

Only by uncovering the past and exposing buried feelings to scrutiny and analysis can parents break the cycle. Just look at the way we have learned to deal more openly with the subject of sexuality. The American post–World War II generation was dominated by returning servicemen, whose world travels very much reduced their parochialism, and by young women who had been allowed new freedom outside the kitchen in support of the home-front war effort. These more cosmopolitan couples, forcibly torn from their past, rejected many traditional strictures regarding sex and eased the topic open for discussion and analysis. As a result, their children, the baby boomers, grew up with sexual attitudes very different from those their parents had grown up with. Unfortunately, we haven't made comparable progress in breaking the chain of passed-on attitudes toward some of the other topics this book treats. For many of these, there have been no world upheavals to help us along. Where there has been progress it's only been through the sheer determination of parents, driven by a concern for the well-being of their own children.

Rita was scarred by parents who always labeled her "the smart one" and expected perfection from her in everything she did. Though she clearly saw herself as hobbled by an obsessive perfectionism, she demanded the same commitment to perfection in her children. She failed to recognize the harm she was doing to her children until her daughter finally exploded at her: "I can't be perfect like you!" She then began examining her own perfectionist tendencies, forcing herself to recall how much her parents had pressured her as a child. She is now making an effort to be less judgmental with her own children, allowing them the freedom to be less than perfect in areas where they want no more for themselves.

Nancy is another parent who learned from the mistakes of her parents. She told me that she spent a great deal of her troubled childhood thinking she must never complain. She often heard her mother telling others how strong and resilient Nancy was and that no problem was too great for her to handle. Quite naturally, although she often needed her mother's emotional support desperately, she could not bring herself to ask for it. And, of course, her mother never offered that support. Recently, she was going through family problems of her own, and her son began showing severe signs of stress in reaction to those problems. "At first I thought, he's a sturdy little guy. He can handle it," she told me. "But then I realized I was doing the same thing to him that my parents had done to me. Perhaps he won't be all right." She decided to take her son to a therapist rather than bet his happiness on his sturdiness.

Even the way your family handled the topic of death over so many generations can be explored and changed in your children's generation. As a young child, Mark had been very close to his grandmother. When she died his whole family avoided speaking about her. Every time he'd attempt to talk about her, he was hushed up. Mark's own father died recently and when his children started to talk about their grandfather, Mark cut them off. "I really don't think now is the time for this discussion," he'd say tersely.

Then as he was reading to his four-year-old son one night, the little boy suddenly started to talk about the last time his grandfather had read to him, pointing out the chair they sat in and the book they read. "Grandpa wanted to read me another story, but it was late and he had to go," the little boy said and started to cry. It was only then that the father realized how much his son needed to talk about his grandfather. He now tries to bring the grandfather's name into conversation, recalling with his son the many happy times the three had had together and recalling some of his father's favorite expressions and habits. Unwittingly, he now understands, he had been protecting himself at the expense of his son. The paradox is that closing oneself off emotionally is no protection at all. Opening himself to the feelings provided Mark personal relief, as well as being a great help to his children.

As these stories demonstrate, your visceral reactions to painful situations your own children are exposed to often have a great deal to do with long-suppressed memories of your parents' handling of similar situations. In fact, some psychologists think that you actually reexperience your childhood by seeing your own children grapple with situations you once had to cope with. Watching the scared look on your child's face as you and your spouse have a loud argument, for example, may reactivate your pain-filled recollections of your own parents' fighting. One would think that in the very moment when a parent is reliving these old, painful moments he would instinctively focus on sparing his own child a dose of the same. Unfortunately, we humans can be unthinking when we are in pain.

But if you aware of what you are feeling and why, you may be able to turn the reliving into a therapeutic experience for yourself. As you observe your children struggle with difficult situations, you can use the feelings that surface to work through some of your own unresolved problems. Once you are able to identify those impulses that come out of your distant past, you can with care and caring constrain yourself to behave toward your children in ways that serve their current needs rather than some old, unresolved issues out of your own childhood.

Furthermore, you may come to better understand the pressures your own parents were under and start the process of forgiving them. Now that you're a parent, you know that no one can spare his child from all pain. Perhaps your parents, within the values of their time, and the understanding available to them, couldn't have spared you that one moment out of your childhood you recall with the most bitterness.

This does not mean that you cannot do things differently, or that your kids will not be better off for your tries to do just that. The philosopher George Santayana once said, "Those who cannot remember the past are condemned to fulfill it." If he were alive today and involved in child psychology, he might take his observation one step further and add that remembering your past may not be enough. To avoid fulfilling (that is, repeating) with your own children the mistakes your parents made in dealing with you, you have to examine what they did, analyze why they most likely did what they did, and understand the forces driving you to do the same.

Then you need to choose a new way of dealing with your children. In each of the chapters that follow, I'll suggest new patterns of behavior to replace the old ones. I'll also explain why these new ones work.

Once you've learned new ways of coping, you'll be less likely to fall back on undesirable parenting techniques you learned by example when you were too young to know better.

3
Through the Eyes
of Children

In the busy lives of all parents with young children, there will inevitably be many stress-filled moments. Parents argue or have money problems, or one of their own parents gets sick, and children may be exposed to scenes they don't understand. As we discussed in Chapter 2, how parents deal with such moments depends on a great number of factors, including their present circumstances and the kind of childhood they themselves had.

You may believe that your children view the factors that cause stress in your family in much the same way that you do. But the truth of the matter is that children see money problems, sexual matters, parental arguing, divorce, death, and other adult concerns in ways markedly different from the way adults do.

Aside from these differences in perspective between parent and child, there will also be many differences from one child to another. These will be related to several factors:

- The ages of the children and their developmental stages.
- Their own individual temperaments, which can range from serene to anxious.
- The parents each child is partnered with. Your own temperament, and that of your spouse, and whether each clashes or jibes with your child's temperament—all exert an influence on how your child sees the adult world.

Understanding these differences in perspective, especially when dealing with potentially difficult, embarrassing, or frightening subjects such as sexuality, divorce, and death, can be crucial in determining the kind of help you give your children. They will need help in interpreting many events that occur in their lives in these areas, but your ability to help them will be influenced by your prior understanding of the special ways children of various ages and stages of development would likely view such happenings. When your preschooler's beloved grandmother dies, and he starts pretending that he himself is dead, you need to understand how a child his age views death, so that you don't explode in anger at behavior that is really age-appropriate.

You need to ask yourself how aware your child is of stressful events happening to or around her. You also must consider that she'll absorb and integrate those events into a sense of herself, for a failure to do so could threaten a child's normal development or inhibit her ability to get on to the next stage of growth. Preschoolers, for example, think long and hard about birth, sex, and death. It would be very easy to judge your preschooler against what you know to be the proper behavior for older children and interpret her fascination with these subjects as inappropriate. Communicating your displeasure with her perfectly normal focus can cause her to shut down this exploration so necessary to her development, or to experience confusion or guilt over it. This will lead to an older child who has difficulty dealing with sexuality or death because she wasn't allowed to find her peace with these subjects at an age when it was most natural for her to do so. But by understanding your preschooler and guiding her through this time of great curiosity, you can help her complete this stage in her emotional development and gain the most from it.

Behind all of this exploration, young children are essentially striving to develop a sense of self. You can facilitate this growth best by appreciating the unique ways they are trying to define themselves at each developmental stage.

How Children Develop a Sense of Self

In the earliest stages of infancy, your child does not really understand that he is separate from you emotionally or even physically. Only gradually does he begin to develop a concept of himself as a separate human being. But when he does, a drive begins, as it does in all children, to define, discover, and get to know himself.

Physically, your child begins to work on tasks such as rolling over, crawling, walking, and climbing. He learns to distinguish your face from those of other adults, and he learns to recognize other familiar faces. This process of distinguishing himself from you and others and learning what his body is physically capable of continues through toddlerhood, the preschool years, and into school age. And you naturally make an effort to prepare the environment for your child by providing age-appropriate toys and equipment and babyproofing your house so he can be free enough to explore and still be safe. You also might enroll a child in a gymnastics or other physical education class to help him refine his physical skills and coordination.

Intellectually, a child only gradually acquires the concepts he needs to understand the world around him. As he struggles to increase his mental abilities, his ability to remember things, to acquire language, and to classify all aid him. You help this process move forward by providing educational toys, such as puzzles, games, audiotapes, and books. Although I do not recommend formal lessons for very young children, I do think that reading to them and talking to them a great deal are natural and effective ways of stimulating their intellect.

Simultaneously, there is a social and emotional development going forward as your child gradually begins to learn about her various feelings. Parents can facilitate the process by helping the child to label the feelings correctly. I cannot stress too strongly how important this is, especially concerning the topics I'll cover in this book. Many children have never learned to label the maelstrom of feelings they have and consequently cannot easily identify or fully understand many of them. And you may not have these skills either, because of the way you were raised. I have counseled adults who don't know when they're angry because when they were small their parents didn't allow them to express those feelings, let alone identify them.

Labeling a child's feelings helps him to realize that his strong emotions are valid and real. When a child explodes in anger at you or a sibling or friend, your natural reaction might be to punish his actions. Obviously, he shouldn't bite a friend or scratch a sibling or punch you. But in explaining that hurting others is not the way to deal with anger, you have to be careful that you do not communicate that it is the anger that is wrong. You also have to be able to offer an alternative to fill the void. If your child had enough vocabulary, he might ask you, "If I can't hit and hurt, what am I going to do with all this power and energy my anger has given me?"

It is very important that you spend time giving your child the freedom to express strong emotions, and a permissible means to do so. You might say, "If you feel like exploding with anger, you can let your brother know how you feel. Tell him that you are furious that he broke your truck." Let your child know that it's okay for him to raise his voice in anger.

Anger isn't the only emotion you need to help your child learn to label. Telling your child she really doesn't dislike Aunt Flora, for example, when actually she does dislike her, will just confuse her. You might say instead, "I know you don't like Aunt Flora and that's okay. You don't have to like everyone you meet. But to be polite, you shouldn't tell Aunt Flora you hate her because it would hurt her feelings. So come and tell me instead. I promise that I won't force you to spend a lot of time with her."

Among the other strong emotions you can help your child label are fear, hurt, pain, anxiety, and sadness. All of these feelings may surface when you and your children are grappling with the subjects discussed in this book. In each chapter on a specific topic, I will suggest age-appropriate ways to explain your own feelings to children, as well as to help them label what they themselves are feeling.

Your children's development of a sense of self has an unquestionable impact on their curiosity about and confusion over all of those sensitive areas I'll cover. As a child becomes fascinated by his or her own body, questions about sexuality may surface, for example. As he begins to understand the difference between fantasy and reality, the finality of death may make more sense. And as she makes and breaks friendships at school, she may develop a new perspective on the arguing and fighting she sees going on at home. Your factual explanations of adultlike events and your proper labeling of the strong feelings these events elicit will profoundly affect the way your children develop both an intellectual and an emotional sense of themselves.

The Role of Temperament

A particular event can have different effects on different children, depending on their temperaments. What is traumatizing to one may be relatively meaningless to another. I've seen some kids go through hair-raising experiences early in life and yet emerge into later life relatively unscathed. Other kids can be terribly upset and thrown off track by the smallest of stresses.

Which personality traits are inborn and which are acquired through the early years of life is still a bit of a mystery to those who study children. We can't really put a percentage on how much of a child's temperament or personality is inborn and how much is acquired. But many parents have told me that as soon as they had more than one child, they realized how much of a child's temperament is present from birth. And some scientific studies into certain temperamental characteristics show that personality differences are apparent in the first months of life. Shyness, for example, has now been shown through some intriguing studies to be an inborn characteristic, rather than learned or acquired. That may be a relief to some parents who worry that it was something they did that caused their children to be overly reserved or wary.

Regardless of the origin of such differences, you owe it to your children to take their temperaments into account when guiding them through the difficult times and uncomfortable feelings that so often surround the topics of this book. If your son is a worrier, for example, be careful not to trivialize his concern when you've lost your job and are searching for another. If your daughter is quick to anger, you may need to be especially diplomatic in your explanations of family arguments. If your child is shy or fearful, you'll need to consider carefully how to handle a memorial service and a funeral, for example. Of course, you will also need to take into account your child's age and intellectual grasp of what is happening. Your own demeanor through the family difficulty must also be factored in.

When Parents and Children Have Different Temperaments

Regardless of how children acquire their personality traits, parents must understand how their own temperamental traits influence the way they deal with their offspring. This is especially true if you and your child have very different temperaments. You must be careful that you don't try to impose your own temperament, which seems so perfect for you, on a child whom it may not suit at all. Forcing a shy child into a situation he obviously finds uncomfortable because you have no difficulty dealing with it substitutes your own needs for your child's. Attempts to help your child overcome his shyness by trying to get him to adopt your more outgoing ways will lead him to mislabel his feelings. "I feel uncomfortable about all this," the child will wonder, "but Mom doesn't, and she says I shouldn't. How do I really feel?"

The reverse of this problem can also occur. A child who

is inquisitive and outspoken, for example, would perplex you if you are the type who has a certain difficulty in talking about delicate topics such as sexuality and death. Her incessant questions could fluster and embarrass you, with the possible eventuality that your bristling, or even just your inability to answer her questions quickly or smoothly enough, would lead her to start curbing her normally exuberant ways. In this situation, you need a way of dealing with her pressing inquiries that acknowledges the legitimacy of her bubbling curiosity but also gives you some breathing time to prepare your responses. Something like the following might be a useful approach: "I'm really not sure how to explain it right now, but let me think it over and then we can talk about it again."

Whatever the personality mix between you and your child, you should take your child's temperament into account when expressing your views through example or discussion. Doing this shows that you respect the child's developing sense of self.

How Toddlers, Preschoolers, and School-Age Kids View the World

As children move through developmental phases from toddler to preschooler to grade-school child, their perception of the world around them changes, as does their understanding of it. Here's a look at what drives children in each of the three age groups.

Toddlers

The toddler lives in an action-oriented world. Her physical self is of the utmost importance to her. Unless you are there to guide her, she can get into some trouble as she strives to gain mastery over her ability to walk, climb, jump, and otherwise use her body. Along with your watchful eye, the toddler needs encouragement and support, expressed by your applauding her efforts to keep her exploration going. Though she cannot yet comprehend much about the stress-filled events that intrude on family life, your reaction to these same events will have an impact on her through this developmental stage. If she's involved in exploring, climbing, and doing, and you're depressed, distracted, or hung over, you won't be available to provide her the aid she needs through this period of rapid growth.

At this age particularly, children need a lot of affirmation about what they are doing and who they are becoming. They need your validation of their newfound mastery of the world. Without this, they may be discouraged from progressing out of this stage in their development and into the next.

As a toddler turns outward to explore his physical world, you'd expect that he'd also gain rapidly in his feelings of empathy toward other people. But the reality is that it's too much to expect this of a child so young and so egocentric. A mother I know told me that her two-year-old son cried for hours on the occasion of his grandfather's death. She was convinced that he understood the significance of what had happened and was mourning the loss of his grand-father. To me, it seemed more likely that his grief was related to how distracted and upset his mother had become. He may have sensed that something strange and unpleasant had occurred, but more important to him was that he had stopped getting the attention he wanted from his mother, a change he had no reason to believe was only temporary.

A toddler will express his anxiety about a stressful event even if he doesn't understand the meaning of the event or its cause or future dire consequences.

On the emotional level as well, a toddler is negative and oppositional, which can have a further impact on how you deal with him during stressful times. For example, if you and your spouse are squabbling a great deal, or going through some major family problem, your toddler's incessant contentiousness on matters that could be of interest only to a child his age will drive you crazy. The more serious the problem you're facing, the less likely it is that you'll have the necessary resources or patience to deal constructively with this and other common toddler traits.

Intellectually, a toddler has very little notion of logic. He may eat alphabet soup, then vomit because he's coming down with the flu, and never want to eat alphabet soup again. He'll be convinced that it was the soup that caused him to throw up. This lack of understanding about cause and effect is common to the age. Jean Piaget, the noted Swiss childhood-development researcher, described a similar situation when he told of the three-year-old who believed it was the swaying and moving of a tree's branches that made the wind blow. This lack of understanding may cause a toddler to believe that his accidental spilling of the milk, for example, is what is causing you and your spouse to argue, when actually your disagreement has nothing to do with him at all. This same sort of logic prevails throughout the preschool years as well.

Preschool-Age Children
Your preschooler is becoming physically and emotionally more separate from you. As her world expands she devel-

ops a better sense of herself as a unique entity within that world. She has friends now and can play some organized games and follow rudimentary rules. But the preschooler is still likely to be quite egocentric, so she'll still need help understanding things from a point of view other than her own. It's at this age, however, that you may see the beginnings of empathy, the ability to understand the feelings and emotions of others. If a friend or a parent gets hurt, she may try to comfort that person. If you are upset over the death of a close relative, or because you've lost your job, your preschooler is likely to be more troubled by your distress than a toddler.

On the other hand, a preschooler's ability to grasp language, feelings, and ideas is growing, too, so there's much more that you can explain to the child. While an explanation of death would be lost on a toddler, the basics of what it all means can be presented to your preschooler, but don't expect him to get it completely. He still lives in a magical world where wishes can come true and fantasy can become reality—the reason a preschooler can be so frightened by monsters and dragons and other such imaginary things. He may wish for his dead grandfather to come back to play with him and finally come to anticipate such a visit as if it were actually in the family's plans. One four-year-old I know continues to refer to visiting a grandmother who has recently died and has told his teacher that both his grandparents are coming to visit him for the holidays. This wishful thinking is sometimes seen by parents as a willful refusal to accept what has been told them. Learn to see it instead as a characteristic of the age.

Logical thinking is still shaky in this age group. If you and your spouse have a sharp dispute one evening or your preschooler sees you upset over some other matter, he may believe that this event caused some unrelated event the next day.

Ironically, along with this absence of logic goes an absence of a figurative sense, and preschoolers can be very literal, taking the things you say at face value. Figures of speech are confusing and puzzling and may lead to huge misunderstandings. Phrases such as "I'm going to kill myself," "Step on it!" and "That makes me sick" can be truly alarming to preschoolers because they take them literally. The same goes for the subtleties of sarcasm. "That was really *very* nice of you" or "Thank you *so* much" said in a nasty tone will baffle them. Are you saying thank you or not?

As mentioned earlier, another common developmental feature at this age is an intense interest in sex, birth, and death. Preschoolers want to know how babies get inside their mothers and how they get out. They're curious about how life begins and ends and want to look at each other's bodies.

And, finally, preschoolers are focused on imitating their parents. This focus will have a powerful impact when it comes to the topics addressed in this book, because it's at this stage of development that children really begin to imprint behavior they see in their parents, and a parent's mannerisms, expressions, choice of words, and ways of dealing with uncomfortable or troubling experiences will become a standard of comportment for the child. A preschooler's personality is taking shape like never before, and it's a perfect opportunity for you to provide a model for solving problems and resolving disputes through reasoned approaches. If you allow anger to enter into every difficult moment, for example, you may find your child doing the same. This is a stage where they're learning to identify with your values, attitudes, and behaviors. They assume you want them to do so, so be careful about the examples you give them.

Young School-Age Children

The school-age child has an even more sharply defined sense of himself as a separate person, recognizing differences between himself and other people quite clearly. At the same time, intellectual concepts that were so difficult to understand earlier are becoming easier to deal with. The basic elements of logical thought will now be present, such as cause and effect and the orderly progression of events. His concepts of time and space are improving dramatically, too. Of course, he's also learning to use numbers and to read, which increases his feelings of mastery and his understanding of the world and himself.

The school-age child will also have much more experience with social relationships. There are school friendships, cliques, clubs, and other activities. These will give the child insights about love and relationships in general that may help her to understand her parents' relationship. She will also have more sympathy toward you if a grandparent or a close friend of yours dies, and will come to realize that not all homes operate the way hers does. She may begin to take notice of how her friends' parents behave toward each other and toward their children. A young school-age child has an intense desire for order and ritual. He likes things to be predictable and organized. If his parent is coping with illness, job loss, or a substance-abuse problem, he will need reassurance and explanations as to why his orderly life is being disrupted. A failure to provide them will distract or derail him from his attempts at industriousness, mastery, and competence in school. He'll react either by not being able to invest himself fully in school, or by investing himself too much in an attempt to blot out the threats to stability he sees or senses at home.

What Children at All Three Stages Need to Feel Secure and Develop Normally

As children go about the task of developing and learning about themselves and the world around them, they need parents who are available to them emotionally and intellectually. They have to have an environment in which they feel safe and secure, where there are regular bedtimes, a desk to work at, and a place for them to put their puzzles and toys. Children need to feel safe—safe in your love for them and safe in the world. They shouldn't have to worry that their world is coming down around them while they're concentrating on their multiplication tables or playing with their blocks. They need regular positive reinforcement that their explorations are worthwhile and praiseworthy, whether it's a toddler climbing the stairs or a second-grader learning the piano.

The extent to which a parent is able to see a child's world through that child's eyes depends very much on the parent's ability to appreciate the differences between herself and her child and to respect those differences. Your own children need you to accept them for who they are, not who you would like them to be.

If during the stressful times brought on by the delicate topics covered in this book parents are unavailable or emotionally preoccupied, or find themselves reluctant to put their own needs aside for the time necessary to enter into the world of their children, they will be unable to meet their children's very real needs. Though it may be terribly difficult for parents to attend to their children's emotional and developmental needs during times that may be threatening to the parents themselves, the healthy development of their children requires that they make every effort to do so.

4
Arguing: Fighting the Good Fight

You arrive home at 6:30 p.m., exhausted and hungry after spending eight hours at work. You can't wait to have that dinner your husband promised to warm up, and then to lounge in the living room your daughters promised to tidy up. But when you step inside the house you find your husband sprawled out on the sofa, sound asleep. Your daughters, their hands all chocolate-smudged, are contentedly playing with their toys—*all* their toys—so that you literally have to use your foot to carve out a path to the kitchen, where not a morsel of food is being warmed. You see *red*.

You storm back into the living room and roughly awaken your husband, accusing him of being both selfish and lazy. You let him know that the kids are filthy, that there is no dinner for you, and that he's a terrible husband and a worse father. Your anger launches you into a litany of complaints about his behavior. You say many cruel things you don't entirely mean.

Your husband tries to apologize, but you're too angry to listen. He tries to tidy up, but you inform him, loudly and in no uncertain terms, that it's too late. He retaliates by snapping back at you and reminding you of the many ways you've failed him in the past.

Now the children enter the fray. Your four-year-old, who has been sitting frozen in silence, bursts into tears and begs for forgiveness while clutching you around the knees. At the same time, your seven-year-old grabs the toy nearest her and runs off to her room with a look on her face somewhere between fear and disgust.

You immediately feel a rush of anxiety and remorse at the sight of your upset children. You worry that the kids will think their family is disintegrating. You start to consider the possibility that your frequent arguments with your husband may be at the root of the recent tendency of your daughters to fight not only with each other but also with their friends. And you wonder if all this fighting could be the cause of your younger daughter's recent nightmares.

In a sense, all the chapters that follow this one involve principles similar to those brought into play by parental arguing. Whether the issue is money or debt, substance abuse, sex and nudity around the house, or dysfunction in the marital relationship, couples under stress are ripe for disagreement. Even a serious illness or death in the family can cause a sudden disruption of the harmony between the parties to a marriage.

No matter the subject of the disagreement, however, there are ground rules you can learn that will help your children develop their own sound ways to deal with disputes.

What Children Learn
from Seeing Their Parents Argue

Arguing in front of a child need not be a catastrophe for the child. It's how you disagree and how you resolve things that makes the difference between a destructive or a constructive experience. The fact is, kids need to see that their parents may not always be of the same mind, that people who differ, even angrily, can continue in a loving relationship, and that positive outcomes can be reached through a full airing of the points of conflict between two people— in short, that it's okay to argue with a loved one, and that one can do so without risking the love of the other person. Children have to come to understand that conflict will be part of everyone's life at some time, including theirs. Allowing your children to witness parental disagreements (constructive ones, of course), and then letting them see how compromises are reached, teaches them that both parties in the argument matter and that people who love each other can find workable solutions to their problems.

No conscientious parent sets out to undermine a spouse, to snipe, or to stage an argument in front of the children. Most resolve to argue discreetly, late at night, or when the children are visiting friends. But arguments can erupt spontaneously, often at inopportune times—over dinner, in the car on the way to Grandma's house, at the store where you're buying a new school wardrobe. Just the fact that so much of a couple's life is spent in front of their children assures that at least some of the disputes between them are going to occur in front of the children.

Nearly half of all parents admit that they have argued in front of their kids. The most common subjects of these arguments are: children (especially discipline), money, the amount of attention spouses pay to each other, and the division of responsibility in the household.

The more impersonal an argument, the easier it is for children to brush it off without suffering any lingering effect. Disagreements over the views of political candidates, for example, or whether America should interfere in the Middle East, are relatively unimportant to a child. The more personal the points of conflict, the scarier they become for the children. "You're a lousy father" or "Why don't you stop being so lazy and go get a job" or "I'm sorry I ever married you" are the kinds of fighting words that trouble kids most. Such personal attacks cause kids to believe that their parents are at war, and that the dispute will not be resolved except through damage to one parent or the other, or to the relationship between them. And once a child comes to believe that his parents may not remain together, the world is no longer a safe place for that child.

The Child's-Eye View

Think back to how you felt as a child when you heard your parents arguing. Many people recall that even minor or momentary bickering between their parents, even over seemingly trivial topics such as "Why do you want to see *that* movie?" or "Not meatloaf for dinner again!" caused them to feel some degree of uneasiness. And their discomfort increased as parents' tempers became more heated and the words louder. Few remember how the arguments were resolved, and almost none remember their parents coming to talk to them about what they had seen or heard. Instead, they were left alone with their fertile imaginations, conjuring up scenarios far worse than the truth.

Exactly what goes through a child's mind when he has

witnessed his parents shouting angry words at each other depends in large part on the age and maturity of the child. Let's take our three developmental stages—toddler, preschooler, and young school-age child—and see how a child in each stage might respond to parental discord.

Toddlers
No child is too young to escape being distressed by the sound of his parents in a serious shouting match. First, of course, children of all ages want their parents to be a unified, indivisible team. Second, in the child's view, parents are supposed to be steady, stable, objective, and fair. This is important to children because parents have so much control over their lives. To see parents lose control is scary to kids because it threatens their own safety and security.

Though toddlers may not understand all the words being thrown back and forth, they can certainly recognize the discord. They react to looks on their parents' faces, their body language, and, of course, the tone of their voices. A two-year-old caught in the crossfire of a raging argument will feel the way a trapped animal feels, desperate to flee but paralyzed with fear, for there is no way for him to escape and no place to escape to. He'll look from one parent to the other and back again in wide-eyed bewilderment. I've seen small children bury their heads in their hands, or in a pillow, or even in one parent's lap, trying to shut out the sights and sounds around them. Some cover their ears, as if to say, "Please, I don't want to hear any more!"

The tension created by repeated noisy, aggressive disagreements can have a cumulative psychological toll on young children, causing them to become very fearful, tightly wound, and easily agitated. Such children may even begin to imitate a parent's argument antics, turning red in the face, pounding on the table, and raising their own voices. Other children of this age who are exposed to a pattern of parental fights will suddenly break out into nervous crying, as if suddenly recognizing a horrible new reality in their lives: that their own personal safety and well-being are no longer assured. This is a very real and very frightening fear for all children who anticipate a possible rupture in the relationship between their parents.

Preschool-Age Children

Children between three and five years old are shocked by a parental fight in much the same way toddlers are, but they are more aware of what the fight is about. They are now able to understand some of the accusations being tossed back and forth and to recognize those themes that tend to recur like angry refrains in fight after fight.

Children this age will try either to interrupt the fight or to deflect their parents' attention away from each other, even if this requires diverting the anger toward themselves. One woman told me about a recent argument she and her husband had had in the car (one of the likeliest and worst places for a disagreement to break out, I might add). They were in the front seat squabbling over the shortest route to the beach. Meanwhile, in the back seat, their three-year-old son began to talk loudly, kick the back of the front seat, and then to hit himself a few times. Their five-year-old daughter, on the other hand, was trying to hug her mother from behind, while pointing out the beautiful flowers along the roadside.

Although they used seemingly opposite strategies, both children were aiming for the same goal: to interrupt the argument by interjecting themselves into it, one by using attention-getting misbehavior and the other by initiating personal contact designed to calm one of her angry parents. I've also seen children start crying, shouting, or screaming in an effort to divert their parents' attention away from each other. And it's not uncommon for one sibling to pick a fight with another one for the same purpose.

Remember, too, that children of this age often take what they hear literally, rather than figuratively, as it was intended. Saying to your spouse, "I'll never speak to you again," may lead a child to imagine a house of silence forever. A child who hears his father say to his mother, "You make me sick," may expect his dad to come down with some awful illness. And perhaps the worst for a child to hear is "I can't stand it here another minute. I'm leaving!" As far as the child is concerned, his paramount fear, abandonment, is about to be realized.

Young School-Age Children

Because kids from six to eight are becoming more socially aware, they have one more concern to add to those they share with their younger siblings: they become embarrassed at the spectacle of their parents fighting. A child can be mortified if her parents are arguing in the background while she's on the phone, or if they display even a hint of discord when she has a friend visiting.

It is natural for second- and third-graders to see events through other people's eyes—those of their classmates, for example, or their teachers—and thus such children would be ashamed if their parents were to be seen by others as having anything less than a properly harmonious relationship. When their parents fight, they worry that everyone

will learn of it, that the next-door neighbors or even someone walking by in the street will get an earful of the awful
things they say to each other. They even fret about *potential*
embarrassment: What if someone happens to come to the
door during a heated argument? One child I worked with
worried that his parents' angry voices, which never even
reached the level of screams, would bring the police to his
door.

Rather than try to intervene in their parents' battles in
an attempt to stop them, children of school age prefer to
absent themselves from the scene, to crawl under the fur-
niture, to simply vanish into thin air. They often feel humiliated by their parents' obvious lack of control.

What's more, these children often feel pressed to take
sides: they feel lost when they're not aligned with someone.
They can be impatient of ambivalence at this age, and so
see such situations in black-and-white terms, with one parent as right and the other wrong, which in turn helps justify
their taking sides. One woman, in the midst of angrily accusing her husband of stingy behavior, watched wide-eyed
as her school-age son jumped into the fray, shouting at his
father, "Yeah, and the last time I asked you for money for
baseball cards, you turned me down, too."

Though I don't believe this particular little boy was doing
so, I have seen school-age children attempt to use the dis-
sension between parents to their own advantage. They
might choose the time of hard feelings between parents
following a fight to ask one parent for a special treat, knowing full well that it's something the other parent would
veto if he or she were consulted. Often this results in the
child's feeling guilty about his blatant manipulation of his
parents.

Why Children Blame Themselves

All children tend to blame themselves for their parents'
bickering. They spend hours trying to figure out exactly
what they did to cause the fight their parents are having.
Because they are egocentric, they assume that actions of
theirs that would seem insignificant to us are capable of
sending ripples of disharmony throughout the family. A
child who left his bed unmade or forgot to walk the dog
may actually believe his act of omission got his mother so
mad she turned on his father. The next step in his fearful
scenario is that his parents will figure it out and turn on
him together.

Even after talking to literally thousands of children, I
am always amazed by the inventive logic they employ to fix
blame on themselves. I have seen children describe with
complete certainty how their parents ended up in a rip-
roaring fight because of some trivial act the children might
have committed, an act the parents probably did not even
recall. If only they hadn't spilled their glass of milk at breakfast, Mommy wouldn't be yelling at Daddy right now. And
what they wish for more than anything is the power to
magically undo their misdeed and put their parents back
at peace with each other.

A man I counseled recently recalled that as a preschooler
he was exposed to nonstop tension between his parents. He
was sure that their arguments were his fault, but try as he
might, he couldn't think of what he had done to cause them.
So every morning, the first thing he did when he woke up
was run to his father and say, "I'm sorry." In logic typical
of a four-year-old, he reasoned that if his father could forgive him for whatever he might have done, or might do,
no new arguments between his parents would start.

How Children View a "Slow Burn"

In some families, arguments almost never erupt into all-out fighting. Instead, they simmer for long periods of time, periodically bubbling to the surface in the form of sniping or sarcasm. In most cases, the anger gets cranked up a notch or two when the right (or maybe I should say, the wrong) button gets pushed. For one overburdened wife and mother, just seeing the phone book left out, or items of dirty clothing on the floor, could set off a string of snide comments. "It's interesting how the phone book never seems to find its way back to the drawer it was removed from." Or: "Isn't it strange that I'm the only one who knows we have a hamper in the house?"

Helen told me that it was her family's weekly visits to her paternal grandparents that angered her mother. She didn't remember ever witnessing a loud argument about these excursions, but rather a series of sarcastic remarks by her mother. "Sunday already? Gee, it seems like just a week ago we were here." Helen's mother never raised her voice or threatened, but she didn't have to. Her sarcasm accomplished all that and more. Though she never seemed to give in to anger, Helen could hear the tension and bitterness in her voice, and she found it very distressing.

Children of all ages find sarcasm and sniping hard to understand. They sense that all is not right, yet they can't put their finger on exactly what is wrong. By not being direct and up front when they are upset about the behavior of a spouse, parents can inadvertently cause their children to doubt their own judgment about human relations. These children are left with a sense of confusion, often unable to label aggressive behavior for what it is. I've heard children deny that the sniping they're witnessing expresses hostility between their parents.

Kids who are exposed to this kind of indirect expression of feelings year after year can react in one or more of several ways. Besides denying the meaning of what they see (and, worse, eventually coming to distrust their own ability to interpret what they see), some adopt for themselves the style of dealing with others they observe in their parents, growing into sniping and sarcastic adults.

Others experience feelings of rejection when their parents turn that same sniping on them. Rosemary recalled for me a day when she was being extremely demanding, asking her mother for a million and one things the way eight-year-olds sometimes do when involved in a new interest. Suddenly, her mother turned to her and totally off the subject snapped, "Can't you do anything with your hair? It looks like a rat's nest. Don't you ever comb it?" Rosemary recalls slinking away to her room feeling diminished and unloved and wondering what had brought on that attack about her hair.

What had happened, of course, was that Rosemary's mother had reached a saturation point with Rosemary's demands, coming as they did when she had many other pressing concerns. But instead of addressing Rosemary's self-absorption directly, she criticized her appearance, causing confusion and hurting her child's feelings. It would have been much better if she had merely stated, "I'm feeling tired and overwhelmed by all the things you want from me today. Let's save some of them for tomorrow, when I know I'll have more time and energy."

Missteps Parents Make

Part of getting things right is learning to recognize our mistakes. Before we can decide how we should talk and behave in front of the kids in various situations, we must recognize what doesn't work. One patient of mine had never thought that her "slow burn" could be as potentially damaging to her children as an all-out demonstration of fury. Once she understood the effect her behavior might have on the children, she resolved to be more open about her feelings, both to her spouse and to the children themselves. Parents who argue in front of their children often make these other common mistakes:

• *Saying "Nothing is wrong" after the kids have seen you arguing.* It does absolutely no good to sweep disagreements under the rug and pretend to the children that everything is fine when it's obvious to them that it isn't. You don't have to be screaming or throwing dishes for your children to guess that you're angry. Anger is expressed not simply through words and actions but also through body language and gesture, the way you roll your eyes, or the tone of voice you use. Some of the fiercest battles between couples take place without a voice being raised.

Such people can deny that they're acting in anger. I've talked with parents who are seething with rage, yet deny it in front of their children. You may think you're protecting your kids from an ugly truth, but few children take such denials at face value, and will either blame themselves for the discord they clearly see around them or imagine that the problem is worse than it is. What's more, if every dispute is subverted and hidden, your kids may grow up feeling that anger is unacceptable and eventually learn to bury their own intense feelings.

• *Pleading your case before your children.* "You saw how Daddy just insulted me!" or "This is exactly what he did three years ago" is never an appropriate statement to make within your child's hearing. What you're really doing is exploiting your child, using her as a sounding board or, worse, as judge and jury in your dispute with your spouse. It's not your child's job to support you or comfort you or fight for you or rule for you.

The fact is, children see their parents as a "package deal," and any attempt to divide their loyalties is misguided. In the process of making an alliance with one parent, the child risks the loss of the love of the other parent. Even if the parent will not hold it against the child, the child may long wonder if the parent really harbors a grudge. If, during any one particular fight your child does take sides, you can be sure he has done it for reasons related to his development and not because he has seen the overwhelming and indisputable justice in your position.

• *Letting children become active participants in the fray.* Children should never be encouraged, or even allowed, to stand in for one of the parents. Liz, a girl I once counseled, recounted terribly vivid stories of fights in her family during which her father raged, often violently, while her mother quivered and remained silent. Unable to bear her mother's seeming inability to defend herself, she stepped into the fray in her mother's place. In fact, Liz took on her father so often that he started to call her "Mother Protector," a name that haunted her throughout childhood and later life.

Being forced to play this role cost Liz dearly, for in order to maintain her role as protector of her mother, she was forced to shut her father out of her emotional life.

Years later, Liz realized that her mother had been less a passive victim than she had seemed. She came to understand how her mother's feigned passivity shared blame with her father's rage for cheating her out of her own childhood and out of her positive feelings for both parents.

• *Trivializing your partner's anger.* A child who witnesses one parent repeatedly diminish the feelings and attitudes of the other will conclude that the second parent needn't be taken seriously. The child learns that as soon as this second parent starts babbling, it's okay to tune her out. Marie allowed herself to be set up for such a response from her husband and the kids. When her frustration with her husband became unbearable (usually over some household chore he had forgotten to do), Marie would often go stomping off to their bedroom in a rage. And she would top it off by slamming the bedroom door—not once, but twice. She did this because the bedroom carpet would stop the door from producing the desired bang and she would have to reopen it, now more frustrated than ever, and slam it again, harder.

But recently, Marie's daughters told her that when she went stomping off that way, their father would vocally count the number of steps it took for Marie to reach the bedroom and for them to hear the inevitable double slam of the door: fourteen for the flight of steps, four more to reach the bedroom, and then, *Bang! . . . Bang!* The three of them would laugh about it, the daughters drawn by their father into a conspiracy against their mother that will surely hurt them one day. Marie's husband managed to trivialize his wife's anger and to justify in the eyes of their daughters his own role in provoking it. He might as well have said to them, "There goes crazy Mom. You know how she gets. If we just ignore her, she'll get over it soon."

When Marie learned of the cruel routine, she was furious at her husband, and for good reason. But she had to face the fact that she, too, had a part in allowing it to begin.

• *Resorting to humiliation.* Arguments that make serious and generalized personal attacks on the other party instead of sticking with what that person may have done are especially insidious, and even more so when they are made in front of the children. Marcia admitted to frequently yelling at her husband in the midst of a freewheeling fight, "You're a poor excuse for a man." In those few words, she managed to degrade her husband in front of their son. However unrealistically, a child will hope for a change in the behavior of one parent that provokes the other in order to bring about an end to the conflict between them. But he cannot hope that a worthless parent will somehow be reborn as a better one.

Inevitably, the disrespect Marcia's son heard in his mother's voice gradually seeped into the tone he now takes with his father, and the relationship between the two has quite naturally deteriorated. What's more, the child has learned that the way to react to conflict is to degrade the person he's arguing with, and he has begun to attack others in this same way his mother attacks his father.

• *Using profanity as a weapon.* Children are great imitators, and any expletives that escape your lips in front of the children will undoubtedly come back to strike your ears, one day soon. Even small children love imitating the profanity they hear adults using. The inflections with which such words are usually delivered alerts children to the fact that they are special adult words and that their use signals maturity. As a consequence, whenever your children want to play grownup, they will trot out these words as props, just as they might put on Mom's high heels. If you don't want to hear repeat performances of your profanity at the most inappropriate times, then avoid using such language yourself.

• *Walking out of the house in anger.* Storming out of the house in anger in the midst of an argument can only invite your child to imagine the worst: that you may never come back—a child's most worrisome fantasy. I had one girl tell me that when her father left the house in a rage, she imagined he had another family that he went to, a sort of duplicate of the one he shared with her, but one where there was no strife to disturb him. Another child feared that when her mother left the house full of rage, she might literally explode or come to some other harm.

• *Resorting to physical violence.* Dishes should stay in the cupboards and books on the bookshelves. And parents should never strike out or make a threatening gesture at each other or their kids. I can't stress this enough, for there are few rules in rearing children as hard and fast as this one. Hitting, or any other display of physical violence, will inevitably teach those who observe it that the way to solve problems is with violence. There is no upside to violence at all, for rather than clearing the air, as some believe, violence immediately destroys trust between people. Further, it trivializes the real reasons for the argument, leaving no impetus for a sensible resolution of the dispute.

Everyone's safety is threatened during a violent, physical fight, and children are especially vulnerable in these moments to fears about their own safety and well-being. One girl told me that during her parents' fights, her father sys-

tematically went about destroying every breakable item he
could get his hands on. She felt certain that one day a plate
or mug would come sailing straight toward her. It was not
an unreasonable fear.

• *Arguing about differences in child-rearing practices in front of
the children.* Because children start out assuming that all
their parents' fights are caused by them, disputes about
child rearing fought out in front of the children confirms
their fears about being the real cause of family disharmony.
When they hear their names come up in angry fights, it's
as though their worst fears had come true. Rather than
loudly berating your spouse for letting the kids watch TV
instead of doing their homework after school, for example,
you should raise the issue in private. Once you have reached
whatever consensus you can between the two of you, you
can present that position to the children as your united
front. This will make it easier to reduce their TV watching,
as well as avoid having them see their behavior as the source
of a fight between their parents.

If children see themselves capable of provoking a division between their parents, they may really be frightened
of the power this seems to bring them. All they have to do
is misbehave and their parents go into spasms of attacks on
each other. Children want to know that even when they
forget for a moment and don't do as they're supposed to
do, a parent will be there to rein them in before too much
damage is done. When adults, who are supposed to be in
charge, are seen as responding to childhood misbehavior
by losing control and lashing out at each other, children
suddenly find a new dimension to the damage their misbehavior can cause. This is too much of a burden to lay on
a child.

New Moves

Conflict and tension exist in the world, and children who don't learn how to handle disagreements within the relatively sheltered and safe haven of their families won't be prepared to handle the many conflicts that are sure to intrude in their own lives as they grow up. You and your spouse should consider the arguments you have, not as calamities in the history of your child's development, but as opportunities for learning. Take the opportunity to teach your children the art of and value in negotiation, and to demonstrate your ability to empathize, your willingness to compromise, and your readiness to apologize for hurt you have inflicted on others.

Do your kids a favor. Start by avoiding the common mistakes I described above and then learn the new moves described below. This will provide your children with a positive model for conflict resolution and help them strive to develop their own pattern of constructive solutions to everyday problems.

• *New Move 1: Acknowledge an argument and encourage your children to express how they feel about it.* Any altercation your child witnesses requires some explanation, no matter how minor or major the disagreement was. Most arguments are unsettling for children, even those you manage to stop almost immediately. First, let your children know that what they saw was indeed an argument, that they were accurate in their perceptions. And, just as important, that you want them to know they can talk about it with you. Reassure them that this is not something that Mommy and Daddy are trying to hide from them. To a child around two years of age you might say, "I think our argument might have upset you, and we're sorry." You can ask a child over age four how she feels about what she saw. And you can add, "I know you just heard Mommy and Daddy screaming at each other, and it was very upsetting for everyone. I'm sorry that we upset you, but sometimes grownups lose their tempers. It certainly wasn't caused by anything you did, and it certainly won't cause either of us to feel any differently about you."

• *New Move 2: Give the children a simple explanation about the content of the disagreement.* The details of your explanation will vary depending on the age of your child, of course. With toddlers under two years of age, you can't do much to undo what they've witnessed. Over time they will begin to see and accept that things have indeed gone back to normal. For kids over two you might offer a simple "Mommy and Daddy don't agree on what we should all do tomorrow, but we'll figure it out. And even when we're angry, we still love each other."

Preschoolers need only as much information as will calm them down. Present the facts in a straightforward, matter-of-fact way. One couple had a heated argument in front of their children about Grandma's insistence that the family come for dinner the next evening. Behind the obvious cause of the fight was the fact that Daddy's mother has always been intrusive, and that Daddy finds it impossible to stand up to her. There is no need to discuss all this with your children. It's more background information than they are interested in or can digest. Instead, you calmly explain, "You know how much Grandma likes us to have dinner together, but I prefer not to go tomorrow. I'd rather go next week." This reassures your child that the content of the disagreement isn't all that threatening.

With school-age children, it's possible to elaborate a bit more on the scenario. You could talk about the fact that Grandma is Daddy's mother, and although he wants to do what Grandma likes, he understands that Mommy has feelings, too.

I find it helpful to explain adult circumstances in terms of analogies drawn from your child's life. You could say to your child, for example, "You know how you feel when Tommy wants you to play baseball and Mark wants you to play video games? You feel pulled in two directions at once, don't you? And that's just how Daddy was feeling."

• *New Move 3: Learn to recognize the real source of your anger and tell your children about it.* In my experience, arguments are more likely to occur when one party or both are feeling frustrated, criticized, disappointed, insulted, or ignored. In other words, some residue of seething anger predisposes toward a confrontation at this time. It's the old "kick the cat" syndrome. Your boss criticizes your work, and you feel frustrated because you're unable to strike back. As soon as you come home you find the cat in your favorite chair and strike out at him. Claire, a friend of mine, asked her husband to be sure to call the plumber about the running toilet. When she got home from work, she asked him if he had remembered to do it. He admitted that he hadn't; an emergency had come up at his company and he just hadn't had the time. Before Claire knew it was happening, she found herself screaming at her husband, "I knew I couldn't count on you for anything! You never come through for me!"

When Claire calmed down, she realized that she had been primed for her outburst by an event that had occurred earlier in the day. A colleague who had promised a report had failed to deliver it, and Claire's boss had held her responsible for the failure, in front of her subordinates. All day, she'd been carrying this frustration around with her, and as soon as she learned of her husband's lapse, she just unloaded on him. Worse, she did so in full view of her now upset and confused children, just as her boss had publicly criticized her.

As soon as you have identified the underlying cause of your anger, admit to it with your spouse and your children. You can say, "This has nothing to do with you. I was angry with someone at work, and didn't let it out until just now. It wasn't your fault at all. I'm sorry."

• *New Move 4: Tell your family when you're feeling cranky.* Whether or not you fully understand the reason for your crankiness, it's important for your family to know how you feel. Everyone has days when she feels out of sorts and consequently walks around with a shortened fuse. Warning those around you can help prevent flare-ups. For those times when a fight erupts anyway, you can still make a graceful exit. "Gee, I'm sorry I ever started this discussion," you might say. "I didn't mean to. I don't know why I'm so grouchy today. But since I am, I think I'll just excuse myself for a little while."

• *New Move 5: As soon as a discussion starts to escalate into an argument, stop it in its tracks and set a time and place for private discussions.* The best way to avoid wreaking havoc with the kids in such a situation is simply to have a plan with your spouse to stop before bellowing another nasty word. If you have legitimate gripes with each other and need to have them out, you can still stop the escalation in its tracks if you have agreed beforehand to respect the need to avoid really angry exchanges in front of the children. You might remind your spouse of your previous agreement by saying, "Listen, this isn't the best place for us to argue. Let's stop now, and we'll discuss it later, alone."

When parents are able to come to their senses in this way, they show their children that angry feelings don't have to get control over people and don't always overwhelm them, and that even if they are displayed, they can be managed so that they do not cause wanton injury to others. If your children witness the tension between parents, but then also see them making plans to resolve the conflicts contributing to the tension, they are helped in learning yet another strategy mature adults use to deal with their anger. Of course, you should always follow up and let them know later that you were able to work out your differences.

• *New Move 6: Explain to your children if you must leave the house during a feud.* Storming out of the house in anger requires a quick explanation to your kids. You must always let them know you'll be back, and when. You could simply say, "I'm really angry and I must cool off for a few hours. I'll be back to tuck you into bed." Or: "I need to go out right now, but I'll see you when I get back." Reassure your kids that you are all right: "Don't worry about me, I'll be fine." This shows them that you are once again in control.

• *New Move 7: Remember to apologize to your kids when you do have a bitter argument in front of them.* Children need to know that adults aren't perfect, and that when they make mistakes they own up to them and apologize. That tells the kids that they can make mistakes, too, and that admitting to them will not cause them to lose your love.

One father reported to me that shortly after he had a big blowup with his wife he gathered his daughters around him and apologized. Their bodies literally went limp with relief. He told them he was so sorry for frightening them and that he and Mommy would work really hard at finding a way to resolve their disagreement. His daughters, he told me, volunteered to help find a solution.

Another woman told me that if her father blew up, he was sure to come back a few minutes after he cooled down in order to apologize. She knew it was coming and knew her father was sincere about it. When children see the same behavior over and over, it becomes predictable and, in this case, comforting.

• *New Move 8: Make sure your children see that vocal and visible disagreements have been resolved.* This is especially important because it goes to the child's worst fear; abandonment by one or both parents. All children, no matter how old, breathe a little easier when they see concrete, physical evidence that a dispute between their parents will not lead inexorably to the breakup of the family. They need to see that although their parents were fuming at each other just a few minutes before about having dinner at Grandma's or over whose turn it was to balance the checkbook, the parents are once again talking in normal, conversational tones and that their parents' faces are no longer taut with anger. In fact, it would be quite helpful for parents to make a point of demonstrating that they've really made up by hugging and kissing each other. Only then can the children rest assured that their personal safety and the integrity of the family are no longer threatened by the blowup.

Older children who have overheard an argument should be given a few details about how you resolved it. You might say, "I know you overheard our disagreement. Here's what we decided to do." Then be specific so your child can understand how grownups compromise in ways that satisfy everyone. For instance, "We decided that instead of having dinner at Grandma's on Wednesday, we'd all go on Monday when Mom's schedule is less rushed."

In this way, children learn that while disagreement may be inevitable, it doesn't have to be destructive, and that people who care about each other can achieve workable compromises. You have the ability at such times to provide a guide for your children through some of life's most difficult future moments by showing them that conflict is not only a natural part of life, but also an opportunity for growth and change.

5
Sex and Nudity

When you arrive at school to pick up your child from his prekindergarten class, his always cheerful teacher beckons to you. She's not smiling as she asks, "Can I have a few words with you?" You ask a friend to keep an eye on your son while the children play in the schoolyard. The teacher tells you that your son is spending an inordinate amount of time talking about penises, vaginas, buttocks, and other private body parts. "He's not using slang. He knows all the correct terms," she says, smiling now. "Many children his age do have a fascination with sexual body parts and love to talk about them. But I think he's doing it excessively."

Mortified and just slightly shocked, you walk back into the schoolyard. You've promised the teacher that you'll talk to your son, but secretly you wonder if you're to blame. For some time now, you've noticed him staring at you and your husband as you both get dressed in the morning. The television is in your room and he watches a children's show there, but now you wonder if he's really there to watch the show. He still bathes with your husband sometimes, too. You've always assumed it was okay. After all, you and your husband are part of a generation that accepted the human body as a thing of beauty, not shame, and you want your child to feel that way, too. But now you feel confused and conflicted. He's obsessing on this stuff like a little sex maniac, you think darkly. What if he does this when he visits friends? Does he do this in front of his babysitter? You're so embarrassed you could die.

What Children Learn about Bodies and Sexuality from Their Parents

Parents can do a great deal to help a child develop healthy sexual attitudes. Seeing that their parents are attracted to each other sexually teaches kids that it's okay to have sexual feelings toward another person. Nonetheless, parents often worry about how much of this sexual interest a child should witness. Part of this concern is about whether it's okay for a child to see a grownup naked.

Because of the hectic lives we lead today, you may not have given much thought to how often your child sees you undressed. You run from the bath to your room in a hurry. You and your child shower together because it's quicker and easier. You let your child into the bathroom with you because of the fuss she raises if you leave her outside.

But children very quickly become aware that genitals are special body parts, not quite like a finger or a knee. They're naturally very curious about their own and their parents' bodies. You like to believe this interest is healthy and wonder what liberties you should allow your young children where your body is concerned. You may wonder if you should permit your child into the bathroom with you, or whether you can harm his sexual development if he sees too much. Parents seem particularly concerned about the possibility of sexually overstimulating young children, and what doing so might mean for the children's eventual sexual development. All this indicates that parents need to be thoughtful in their approach to sexuality and nudity in regard to their children.

In this chapter, you'll learn about your child's evolving sexual feelings. You'll find out about the strong, positive effect you can have on your child's developing sexuality by the way you handle body privacy and adult sexuality. And you'll learn how you can instill in your child healthy attitudes about sex without using yourself and your spouse as graphic examples.

The Child's-Eye View

Think back to the time when your child was an infant. There were probably times when you felt that your body was no longer your own. You may remember having to hold the baby everywhere you went. Or maybe you recall late babyhood and early toddlerhood when your child poked you, pulled at you, and sucked on your fingers and your face as she began to explore her world. Or maybe what's most vivid in your memory are those periods of separation anxiety (which may still be going on!), when your child clung to you whenever you tried to separate yourself from her.

At the very beginning, an infant doesn't realize he and you are separate entities. Then, even when he does, he still feels he has the right to intimacy with your body. As parents, we encourage that. After all, hugging and holding and touching are ways we help a baby feel secure and loved.

You were quite intimately involved in your baby's body, too, if you think about it. You had occasion to peer into every orifice as you changed countless diapers and bathed, massaged, and rubbed cream and powder all over that warm, soft baby body.

But as your child gets older, that intimacy naturally begins to change. A mother who is still nursing may start to feel uncomfortable if her toddler climbs up and reaches under her shirt. You no longer spend all the time you once did changing diapers, especially as a toddler starts toilet training. As you afford your child more privacy, you also begin to teach your child that she can't simply poke, pull at, and suck on you randomly.

Let's explore what children in our three developmental stages are thinking about their bodies and their parents' bodies. You may also wonder how much sexual feeling and awareness they have at these ages. Learning the answers to these questions will help guide you as you begin to decide how much parental nudity and sexuality is okay in front of your children.

Toddlers

For the tremendously active toddler who is running, climbing, and learning how to use his growing body, clothes are simply an encumbrance he'd rather be rid of. You probably know from experience how much toddlers love to take off their diapers, for example. In fact, many toddlers will take off all their clothes at the drop of a hat. One mother told me her daughter wriggled out of her pajamas every night after being tucked into bed. When the parents came up to check on her, she'd be sprawled out, fast asleep and completely nude, no matter what the weather. Sometimes social concerns can cause parents to be uncomfortable when their toddler engages in such behavior, especially when he does so in a public place, such as at the beach. But it is really very innocent.

Innocence also explains the curiosity toddlers have in their parents' bodies. They are endlessly trying to do things to Mom's or Dad's body—putting their fingers in your mouth, inspecting your teeth, looking in your ears, and so on. A concerned mother recently told me that her sixteen-month-old boy was with her in the bathroom. As she finished up, the child reached for the toilet paper, balled it up, and prepared to wipe his mother! She took the paper and did it herself, which was a good idea. Toddlers imitate everything you do. Since the boy was frequently in the bathroom with his mother, he was merely doing what he had seen her do a thousand times. I would discourage a child who tried to do this, however, just to avoid problems down the line when he gets older. The mother here could simply have said, "Thank you, but I'll do it. You can practice on yourself."

Speaking of bathroom activity, toilet training is another major developmental milestone at this age. It obviously has a lot to do with "private" parts of the body. Toddlers are fascinated to see what their bodies can do and produce. At this age they are more concerned with bathroom functions than with sexier aspects of the genitals, although some masturbation is common. It is only later, during the preschool years, that curiosity about reproduction will begin to manifest itself.

Preschool-Age Children
Preschool teachers over the years have told me that their young pupils are almost universally fascinated by two subjects: birth and death. You may have noticed an increase

in the questions, too. "Where do I come from? . . . How are babies born? . . . How'd I get in there? . . . How'd I get out?"

Often, it doesn't end with questions. There may also be an element of "Look at mine" and "Let me look at yours." Some children like to play doctor. This heightened interest in reproduction and those body parts involved peaks in the preschool years. It is relatively dormant during the grade-school years and returns in full force in adolescence.

The preschooler has changed in how she regards her parents' bodies, too. That innocent poke at your nipple may not be so innocent anymore. Your child knows it's a "special" body part now. You also may find your child staring at your body if you undress in front of her.

Parents often wonder what is going through their preschoolers' minds when they stare at a parent's body. Most of the time what they feel is a sense of puzzlement, or curiosity, because adult bodies are so different from their own. They may wonder if that's what they'll look like when they grow up. Because this is such a "sexy" age, they may also feel a certain excitement at seeing their parents' bodies. At that age, children could begin to feel troubled about the differences between their own and their parents' genitals. One father told me that his three-year-old son looked at his father's penis, then looked at his own and frowned.

Many preschoolers spend more time than before rubbing or playing with their genitals, too. Parents are often hindered by their own embarrassment when they try to describe such behavior. A father once called in to my radio show and, with some difficulty, tried to explain that his daughter was constantly "rubbing up against" part of her high chair. It took me a few minutes to figure out what it was he was talking about. Another mother once told me that her daughter and her friends were wrapping their legs around the top of one of the swingset poles in their backyard, then sliding down. To her astonishment, they told her that they were "getting the good feeling."

We cannot run away from the fact that what preschoolers are experiencing when they do this is a sexual sensation. It does feel good! But it is not the same sensation adults associate with sexuality. Nor does it involve all that the adult notion of sexuality entails. To a child of this age, the issues are uncomplicated. You do something to your body and it feels good. It's only later that those feelings take on increased significance.

Some boys may feel frustrated by involuntary erections. I knew one little boy who was perturbed because he didn't seem to have any control over spontaneous erections. He wondered why this part of his body was doing something without his "permission." If a boy seems upset by erections, he should be reassured that they are normal, healthy occurrences.

Some girls also may feel confused about why they don't have penises. Once they begin nursery school, they probably get the opportunity to see little boys showing off what they can do with theirs, especially while urinating. One mother told me that her little girl spent a lot of time attempting to urinate standing up. I think parents in this situation should reassure their daughters that there is nothing wrong with their bodies. Explain that their bodies are different from boys' bodies and the differences are normal. That's the way they are supposed to be. You may also need to offer some anatomical explanations for your daughter. The mother whose little girl tried to urinate standing up explained to the girl that she also had a tube for urinating—it just wasn't outside her body. That made it a little more difficult to urinate standing up, because she couldn't aim with as much accuracy or do it as comfortably.

Young School-Age Children

As children reach age six, their minds turn in interesting new directions. Though there's still some curiosity about sex and the human body, the intense, almost raw, primitive fascination with bodies and sexuality is now diluted. And when they do direct their thoughts to these matters, it's usually expressed in totally different ways.

One father told me that while he was driving his six-year-old daughter and two neighborhood boys home from school, his daughter suddenly asked aloud, "Dad, what does 'dick' mean?" The boys began to guffaw in the back seat, of course. The father, who had the distinct impression that his daughter was leading him on, answered dryly, "It's a nickname for Richard," and the little girl giggled knowingly. Though as a school-ager she was no longer interested in playing doctor, pulling down her pants, or doing such openly "sexy" things, she did appreciate the wordplay.

Children of this age cope with sexuality in a more abstract way, with jokes, put-downs of the opposite sex, and strong identification with same-sex friends. In fact, the preference for all-boy or all-girl groups may be an effort to put sexual thoughts behind them for a while. They aren't spending a lot of time thinking about sexy stuff, as they did in pre-school. Masturbation abates, too. Instead, young school-age kids are much more into their intellectual and social pursuits. They are busy reading, writing, making best friends, collecting things, and playing sports.

How does the young schoolager think about his mother's and father's sexuality now? In all likelihood, children this age are a little embarrassed by the whole thing. They're

probably dressing in private, and if they think at all about
their parents "doing it," it's probably with some amount of
disgust. Remember that feeling you had as a kid (and may
still have) that you couldn't imagine your parents having
sex together? School-age kids find it easier to think of their
parents as nonsexual.

A father told me about a time he was driving home from
a children's book fair with his two young school-age daughters. He had purchased a children's book that explained
sex, and the girls had fished the book out and were secretly
looking at it in the back seat. He overheard the younger
one say, aghast, "No—not Mom and Dad! Mommy just
wouldn't do that. I know how it really happens. Daddy
sneaks up behind Mommy and tells her that her shoe is
untied. Then, when she bends over, he gets her!" The
thought that her mother might willingly go along with such
an act was so foreign to this girl that she had to envision a
sneak attack!

On Nudity, Sex, and Privacy

Parents often ask me where I stand on the issues of nudity
and sexuality in front of children. I think that when a baby
becomes a full-fledged toddler, at around eighteen months
of age, the parents should begin dressing, bathing, showering, and going to the bathroom in private. You are beginning the slow process of helping, in a sense, to wean
your child away from his attachment to you. As I've said,
children start doing this naturally when they reach school
age, but you should begin sooner to teach your children
that your body is private. As with many other child-rearing
issues, starting early will spare your having to change ingrained habits later. Also, when your preschool child is

going through his "sexy" phase, you'll want to do all you can to help him keep his natural curiosity at healthy levels. If he sees a great deal of nudity, he may become over-stimulated, leading to other negative consequences.

When you guide your child outward toward the world of others, not crowding his memory with too many images of parental nudity or adult sexuality, you're positively affecting his future ability to love others and enjoy sex. There is a connection between an adult's sexuality and what he's seen and experienced as a small child. Your thoughtful approach to these topics isn't just to keep him from being an oversexed preschooler, but to give him a healthy base from which he'll grow up and be capable of loving sexual relationships as an adult. A lingering sense of guilt or shame over sexual memories associated with a parent can interfere with this development.

What Does Overstimulation Mean?

Overstimulation, in the sexual context, is a term for either physical (touching), visual (seeing), or auditory (hearing sounds from his parents' bedroom, for example) sexual stimulation that proves too much for a child to handle or process. We don't know which kids will be most vulnerable to overstimulation. Some children may be very resilient, and with these children things like parental nudity will have little effect. Others will be quite upset by many kinds of overstimulation, and end up having their future sexual attitudes colored by these experiences.

While visual overstimulation is fairly simple to define (a child sees too much parental nudity or adult sexuality), physical overstimulation is a little tougher to judge. Certainly, parents should go on hugging, kissing, and holding their children. But use common sense about other forms of touch. You've probably stopped most of the nibbling on ears and other physical intimacies you had with your child as an infant because you realized that they weren't appropriate for a six-year-old. When you have doubts about any behavior, think about the context in which your touching occurs and whether it has any potential sexual charge to it. Pay close attention to how your child reacts. If she is rubbing up against you and obviously becoming overly excited, you'll need to stop what you are doing. By the same token, remember that it's not abnormal for you to have an occasional sexual feeling toward your child. As long as the awareness is there, you should be able to avoid acting on these feelings in any way with your child.

There are some common signs that will tell you if a child is being overstimulated by visual or physical triggers. A child can begin repetitively talking about genitals or other sexual matters. Others attempt sexual activities in their play. Since all preschoolers do this to a certain extent, your child's preschool teacher will probably bring it to your attention if he's going beyond the norm. You can also observe your child's playmates and compare notes with other parents.

Overstimulation can also lead to another type of reaction. If they are seeing too much nudity or sexual behavior at home, they may be unable to sustain a healthy curiosity about sexual matters and eventually block off any awareness of sexual feelings or thoughts. Such a turn of events can have bad consequences, since it is their curiosity that enables them to gradually accumulate information about their own sexuality. Instead, such children may experience a dwarfed development and put away all interest in the subject. By adolescence, the age when they really should experience a reawakening of sexual interest, they still may be uninterested or even repulsed by sex.

You can understand how this reaction might occur if you consider normal sexual development. A child's first love affair is naturally with her parents. Then she gradually begins the process of making her parents less desirable as sexual objects. Nature has a plan here and society's mores have been developed to support it: the child needs to break that tie, so that eventually she can become interested in someone else. But if her parents undermine the process by disregarding society's rules about body privacy, they can derail her natural efforts to see them in a less sexual context.

Children who are overstimulated at a young age can grow into adults with many problems related to sexuality. They may become promiscuous, using sex to get things, or come to view everyone of the opposite sex as a sexual object. Or they may continue to squash sexual feelings, rendering themselves incapable of enjoying physical closeness. Some adults continue to feel guilty about the sexual feelings they had for their parents, feelings their parents didn't help redirect. The burden of these feelings carried into adolescence and even adulthood is often responsible for many kinds of unreasonable expectations or unresolved issues that are brought to their intimate relationships.

Missteps Parents Make

There's no need to go into an anxiety attack if you think you may have overexposed your kids to parental nudity. You should remember that not all children respond in the same way, so your actions won't necessarily have had a harmful effect. Consider the woman who called in to my

radio show and told me that in the rush to get out to work
one morning, she mistakenly handed the babysitter an
X-rated adult videotape for her son to watch. Luckily, the
child's babysitter heard some pretty lurid sounds coming
from the TV room and went to investigate, finding her
charge watching a preview of the film—with all the sexiest
parts highlighted! While I certainly wouldn't recommend
X-rated tapes for your child's sex-ed course, I was able to
assure my caller that one such event was not likely to do
her child any permanent harm.

Here's a list of common missteps parents may take when
dealing with the issues of nudity and sexuality in front of
the children:

• *Failing to recognize your child's sexual feelings.* Kids do have
sexual feelings and overlooking them can be a real mistake.
If you don't recognize their sexual interests, you won't be
as responsive to their questions or as understanding of the
things they do or say. It's true that small children do not
think about sexuality or their own sexual feelings the way
an adolescent or an adult does, and that their feelings don't
have the mental or emotional overlay they will have later
on. Young children don't experience sexual arousal the way
someone after puberty does, because they simply haven't
gone through the hormonal changes that make such feelings possible. They do have slowly awakening sexual feelings, however, even if they're not the hormonally charged
ones we begin to know during adolescence.

• *Allowing your children too much physical intimacy after babyhood.* Young children must break the intense tie to their
parents, a process that could be derailed if you assume
they're nonsexual and act as if your naked body has no

effect on them. Only if they've managed to break cleanly with their first strong intimacy, the one with their parents, will they be prepared for a healthy sexual maturity.

When a child reaches around eighteen months of age, parents need to begin making their bodies less available, especially when the adult is naked or partially dressed. At some point, you have to gently break it to a child that he no longer has a right to such intimacy with your body. A mother who's weaning her child, for example, may worry that the child will think she's rejecting him. That's especially true if he acts frustrated or angry during the weaning process. "I taught him to depend on my body for sustenance and now I'm changing the rules on him," you might say to yourself. But child rearing is an ever-continuing process of changing the rules, especially when the rearing is done with a recognition that your child will be going through very distinct developmental stages as he grows.

• *Downplaying privacy because you think it will make the naked body seem a source of shame.* In these days of greater enlightenment, we want our kids to feel comfortable about their bodies. So some parents may find themselves reluctant to talk about keeping the body private. But children should begin to learn, even at a young age, that you deserve a little privacy—whatever the reason. In our society, privacy is associated with bathroom activities and dressing, so you are helping to socialize him into how the world operates, as well. Besides, children do invade our lives in a sense, and an agreement with them that there should be such a thing as private time will do both the parent and the child some good. You should at the very least be entitled to the right to go to the bathroom and shower by yourself.

If you are even-toned about your requests for your own

private time, your child shouldn't interpret it in the wrong way, for this time of the child's life is filled with new things he is learning from you every day. If your child continues to burst in on you a lot, you could try some mock outrage: "Excuse me! I'm getting dressed and would like a little privacy." Or: "Come on, now, am I going to have to start locking the door to get a little peace and privacy around here?" Your child will not only get the message; she will soon start imitating both your words and your tone when someone violates her privacy.

Of course, the message is best taught by example, so start giving your children their own privacy. Always knock when they're in the bathroom, or in their rooms with the door closed. At around the age of five or six, kids develop some modesty themselves and will probably begin asking for privacy. Respecting these requests is an important lesson to them in how much you value all people's privacy.

There is a danger that children will get the idea that the body is shameful if you deliver the privacy message the wrong way. If you act flustered or embarrassed while telling your child to leave the room while you dress, or if you lunge for your clothes to cover up when they burst in on you, then, yes, they may get the idea that you see your body as something to be hidden. By the same token, if you react harshly when a child appears naked in the doorway, or tell him that he should be ashamed of himself, you will confirm that you think there's something shameful about his body.

At times, parents adopt relaxed rules about body privacy because they think that doing so will help kids learn about their bodies. But for the many reasons we have discussed, a parent's body is not the proper vehicle for a show-and-tell presentation. Besides, adult bodies are so different from kids' bodies that they learn little about their own bodies from looking at yours, except that there may be something lacking in theirs. It might be better that a child look at a naked friend. Consider the matter from a child's-eye view. Not only are your genitals larger and covered with hair, they look different by virtue of where they are being viewed from. Your genitals are just about at eye level for him, and this may intimidate some children.

• *Assuming that children don't notice you getting dressed or going to the bathroom.* Because bathing, showering, dressing, and going to the bathroom are so naturally functional, parents are often not aware of the show they are putting on for their curious children. You think your child is just sitting there watching "Sesame Street" on your bedroom TV while you're getting dressed. In reality, you're a pretty compelling subject to a four-year-old. Why else would kids think of so many reasons why they just have to be with you during such times? "I'm just looking for my boat . . . I need you to tie my shoe . . . I am so thirsty, I just have to have a drink now." The requests are often accompanied by that sheepish look kids get on their faces when they have ulterior motives for their seemingly innocent actions.

By extending the privacy rule to the bedroom and the bathroom, you'll avoid situations such as the one described to me by Joshua. He was in the tub with his two-year-old son, Robert, when the child reached out and tugged on his penis. Joshua felt conflicted. What should he say? If he reacted too strongly, he guessed, Robert might feel he had done something bad or that some shame should be associated with the penis.

Nevertheless, Joshua wanted to say something. So he said, "That's a private part of Daddy's body," which was a good way to respond, but why not avoid getting into such

situations in the first place? Even a small child might recognize the inconsistencies, for it had already been established in the relationship that parents have to touch
children at times, to change them and to wash them. Robert
might have protested, "You touch mine, why can't I touch
yours?" It's best to avoid situations that could be expected
to lead to such conflicts and difficult explanations.

• *Squelching a child's natural curiosity about bodies and sex.* You
should not ignore or trivialize a child's questions about sex
and bodies. Patronizing statements such as "You'll learn
about that when you get older" or "That's not for children"
or even just changing the subject can make a child feel
there's something wrong with being curious.

• *Losing your cool when a child interrupts sex.* Granted, it's
difficult to maintain your composure in such a circum-
stance. In fact, it may be life's most embarrassing moment.

Kids seem to have an uncanny knack for knowing when
adults are getting intimate, and if your kids wander in on
you, and you find yourself feeling flustered and embarrassed, make every effort to regain your composure. Your
child already senses that's he's interrupted something private. Don't make him feel that he's done something naughty
or, worse, that you were doing something naughty. Often,
children who hear or see their parents having sex suspect
that Mommy and Daddy are hurting each other. If you
raise your voice or get visibly upset, it may reinforce the
idea that unpleasant things were going on and that you are
ashamed of what you were doing.

New Moves

Dealing with a young child's growing interest in bodies and sexuality is still one of the most anxiety-ridden tasks a parent faces. Attitudes toward things sexual are very different now from where they were fifty years ago, and over this time enlightened parents have changed their sensibility about sexuality and bodies. Most parents fear taking any action that threatens to lead them back into old-fashioned and long-abandoned approaches. And kids see so much more sex now on TV, on music videos, and in commercials that parents wonder how much their own children know and how they can regain any semblance of control over their sexual education.

Yet parents can still do a great deal to guide a child through a normal sexual development simply by being there to answer all his questions honestly, without embarrassment, but with some common sense, and by realistically limiting the child's exposure to parental nudity and sexuality. By following these two rules, and the guidelines below, you can help preserve for your child one of the great gifts a good childhood can give a person, a healthy sexual outlook.

• *New Move 1: Show positive examples of how you and your mate feel about each other.* This should be first on your list. It's actually good for children to see some chemistry between you two. From this, they learn that sex is okay, that it's exciting, that it's positive. You would not want to flaunt sex or behave sexually in front of them, but a hint of the magic of sex is healthy and can be reassuring.

Just how much should children witness? I would say that flirting, affectionate kisses, and hugs are fine. Petting and other pretty obvious preludes to sex are not a good idea.

From seeing their parents' attraction to each other, children learn that it's acceptable to have sexual feelings toward another person and are given a model for expressing these feelings in a healthy way. One woman I know recalled that when she was a child her parents fought a lot, but it didn't worry her too much, because she regularly walked in on them affectionately kissing and hugging in the kitchen as they cleaned up after dinner. Though she couldn't fully reconcile the two kinds of behavior, she felt reassured that any two people who obviously felt such warmth for each other were not about to split up, even if they did argue.

Sexual gestures of intimacy between parents convey a great deal about healthy adult relationships. And that's an example worth setting.

• *New Move 2: Answer all your child's questions about sex and body parts clearly and matter-of-factly.* Begin by using proper names and accurately explaining how sex organs function. Your child will be curious about these things, and you should make sure he gets accurate answers. If you don't know the answer to one of your child's questions or you feel embarrassed or awkward, tell him honestly that you aren't sure how to answer the question. Then promise to look it up and get back to him. There are many books for children that guide you in explaining reproduction, sexual intercourse, and other, similar topics. These may be a help in satisfying your child's curiosity.

• *New Move 3: Begin to teach your child privacy rules during toddlerhood.* You don't grab at someone's genitals, just as you wouldn't poke someone in the eye. Though in a certain sense you're discouraging your child from some forms of intimacy with you, you can be sure to remind your child about those positive expressions of intimacy, such as hugging. As with all limit setting, prepare the environment so there aren't temptations every minute to break the rules. You shouldn't get into the shower with your preschooler and expect him to resist the temptation to find out what it feels like to touch your genitals, which are right there at his eye level. Remember, your body looks intriguingly different to your child because you are an adult, whether you're the same sex as your child or not. Be as consistent about privacy rules with same-sex children as with children of the other sex.

• *New Move 4: When privacy is impossible, try distraction techniques.* Don't worry if you don't achieve 100 percent success with privacy rules. That's okay. Occasionally you're going to be in a public bathroom and you'll have to share a booth with your child. Or she'll burst in on you while you're getting changed. As long as you're consistent about privacy rules most of the time, these incidents shouldn't matter. One thing going for you is that most young children are easily distracted, and you might try a technique used by one mother I know: when she has to share a bathroom stall with her son, she gets him interested in the ceiling design, the door lock, or spinning the toilet paper roll. It takes the emphasis off her. Similar distraction techniques can be useful if you have to change with your child in the room.

• *New Move 5: Be sure to have a frank talk with your child after she walks in on you while you are making love.* Never just assume that your child will figure it out, even if you've explained sex to her. For one thing, she may have forgotten. I had a parent tell me that she thought she'd taken care of explaining sex when her daughter was four. But five years later, she realized, to her chagrin, that the child didn't remember a thing!

Also, children may not have thought through or considered actual positions, even if you've explained that Daddy's penis goes into Mommy's vagina when two adults have intercourse. They may wander in and find you not in the missionary position, or having oral sex, and fail to connect what they see with what they were told about sex. Some may conclude that their parents are fighting or hurting each other. It may look to a child like you're wrestling. Then there are the sounds! They can be intense, emotional noises that children don't hear very often, or hear only when their parents are angry.

I would suggest that you wrap something around yourself, get up, tend to your child's needs (a glass of water, comfort after a bad dream), and walk her back to bed. Explain that everything is all right and that you and your spouse were making love.

The next day, your child may have more questions, or you may want to bring up the topic yourself. Discussing it right out in the open is best. Tell your child that you and your spouse were not fighting. Explain again what sex is and that it feels good to parents. Don't be surprised if your child still finds it all a bit inconceivable and maybe a little distasteful. You could say what a friend of mine did: "You know how there are some things you think of as fun, like making mudpies, that I think are yucky? Well, there may be stuff grownups do that you think is yucky, but grownups think is fun. And that's okay." In most cases, you will not have to go into as much detail with a toddler; this is more an explanation for a preschooler or a school-age child.

Your discussion could be a brief presentation of the facts, limited by how much your child is actually looking for at this point. This might also be the perfect moment to bring in your values and to discuss the role of love in a sexual relationship.

• *New Move 6: Give your children your beliefs about the connection between sex and love.* Regardless of your values—whether you think there's always a connection between sex and love, or not—you should impart a value system to your children that includes sexual relations between people. Remember that you're not just discussing mechanics or anatomy. You should discuss sex in the context of human relationships and teach your children that sex is just one of the many dimensions to a relationship. Your long-term goal is to help prepare them for the hormonally charged teenage years, so that they can avoid being exploited sexually, or using sex to exploit others.

• *New Move 7: Explain homosexuality truthfully.* It isn't very likely to come up before school age, but even if it does you can still reveal the basics. Tell your child that while most people fall in love with people of the opposite sex (that's a true statement, not a prejudicial one), some people have the same feeling for members of their own sex. These people are called homosexuals.

This might be a good occasion to tell your children about a gay uncle or friend, rather than keeping such information a secret from children, as many families do. It's better for them to know the facts than to guess at them and wish they had been told sooner. This supposes, of course, that the gay family member or friend is living an openly gay life. If he or she is not, it would not be appropriate to share information on someone else's sexual preferences with your child, especially because you would have to follow up the explanation with an admonition that your child must keep the information secret.

If your child seems curious about how two men or two women can have sex (because of what she has been taught about heterosexual intercourse), you can explain that there are many different ways of having sex. Then ask your child how she thinks two men or two women would make love. Her answers may surprise you and/or give you insight as to her understanding of the topic. Tailor your response to her level. Remember that many schools have programs now that explain AIDS and the various ways the virus can be transmitted, so be aware of the information she may have heard.

You should point out the prejudice and bigotry in words like "fag" or statements like "Oh, you're so gay." Ask them what they think is so bad about being gay? It's a different lifestyle and they don't have to like it or think it would be enjoyable—but they should respect the right of homosexuals to live as they choose to live. Remember, telling a child about homosexuality won't cause a child to become a homosexual. Many homosexuals recall feeling different very early in childhood. They later recognized these early feelings as a first awareness of their different sexual orientation.

• *New Move 8: Explain sex for sale.* A father I know was driving past a particular district in New York City with his daughter, when she shouted, "Look, Daddy, that lady's dress is open all the way down the front!" The father, caught by surprise and flustered, quipped, "That lady must have been in such a hurry that she didn't take the time to get completely dressed this morning!" The best route would have been honesty, for questions that come up spontaneously can provide opportunities to explain difficult matters to your child without the intimidating formality that often accompanies sit-down sessions. This father could have told his daughter quite casually that some people have sex with people who pay them to do it, and that it's called prostitution, and that prostitutes often dress in certain ways to communicate that this is what they do. Explain that it is illegal and put forth your views on the topic. Tie your explanation into earlier discussions about the role of sex in a relationship. If your child asks why a person would sell sex, you can talk about the psychological factors, or the role that drugs can play in making people financially destitute and yet unable to hold a normal job, so they sometimes feel they have to turn to prostitution. You might also discuss the risks to both the prostitute and the customer. Make sure they understand that with the help of family, friends, and sometimes public institutions many of these people straighten out their lives to the point where they can leave the life of prostitution.

6
Marriage in Crisis
and Divorce

Ted and Joan had been up for hours the night before, arguing bitterly. They were still angry the next morning when their four- and six-year-olds bounced onto their bed asking for orange juice and breakfast. A pall hung over the breakfast and continued as they piled into the car for a day trip to the beach. As the morning progressed, the children grew increasingly quiet, sensing the intense animosity between their parents.

"I'm not sure how long we can go on like this," Joan said to Ted in a low voice as they were pulling up to the beach. "I just don't know what's going to happen."

Their six-year-old daughter bolted upright in the back seat. "What's going to happen? Where are you going to go, Mommy?" she begged tearfully.

Whether you and your spouse are trying to work through a serious crisis in your marriage or have made up your minds to separate or divorce, the threat to your marriage cannot remain hidden from your children. Kids see you as a package, an amalgam they don't even realize can be separated. It's not unusual for a four-year-old to imagine that his parents were always together, even in childhood. In fact, kids are often mildly shocked to learn that Mom and Dad have different interests, different likes and dislikes. So when the package starts to come apart, the very foundation of a child's emotional world threatens to shatter with it.

Though many couples tend to see the period from the separation to the divorce as the most traumatic for their children, some studies have shown that the immediately prior "marriage in crisis" period can cause problems nearly as serious. Children living with a threatened dissolution of their home life show severe signs of stress, many experiencing new difficulty concentrating in school, and others undergoing disturbing changes in sleeping, eating, and mood patterns. Fighting between siblings may increase. Toddlers and preschoolers may not always be able to identify the nature of the threat hanging over them through this crisis period, but they sense that something is now seriously amiss in their lives.

"My wife and I spent a year of our marriage either crying or yelling every single day. It was so open and so obvious that we had lost emotional control of our lives," said one father. "Even our four-year-old started crying over every little thing."

"My husband would get so angry during our fights that our children grew frightened. I seemed to be spending all my time with them assuring them that their father would eventually calm down," another mother recalled.

If a divorce does occur, your children's already stress-fractured world can shatter even further. Whether children react to it with shock, bitterness, or quiet sorrow, divorce is guaranteed to be a wrenching experience, even if they've grown accustomed to regular fights between their parents. No matter how much turmoil accompanied family life while the marriage was in crisis, children find the finality of divorce almost impossible to accept. And many children will not just sit and cry quietly at the news. At the moment she was told, one four-year-old let out an agonizing scream her father will never forget. A six-year-old became so angry that her mother found it impossible to control her.

A common aftermath of serious marital problems is that, at least temporarily, children lose a sense of security in the relationships they have with their parents. It is vitally important that you think through what you say in front of the children at these times, because in their vulnerability they can so easily misinterpret information being transmitted. You start to lecture your five-year-old son over a childhood mishap, and he asks you, "Do you hate me? Are you going to leave me, too?"

Of course, children can be helped to understand why Mommy and Daddy could not get along. But it is a complex journey for children, from witnessing the first big fight between their parents, to learning that a divorce or separation is imminent, to the day when they first start to accept the reality of it. There will be countless questions along the way, especially from very young children. "My girls had so many questions, and some of them were tough and painful to answer," remembers one woman whose divorce took place two years ago, when her children were four and six. "Once, after I'd reassured them that their father still loved them, they wanted to know: 'But what about you, Mom? Who loves you?'" Other children may clam up and find themselves unable to tell you what they're feeling and fearing.

This chapter will help you develop language with which

you can tell your children what they need to know about your marriage problems. But first, let's look at that universal question that gnaws at parents in crisis marriages: Is it better for children to have two parents putting on a show of unity for the sake of the kids when they really despise each other? Or would the kids be better off if you were up-front about your discord?

Should Parents Put On an Act to Protect Young Children?

A woman I know was arguing bitterly with her husband over whether or not they should continue to pretend in front of the children that things were all right between them, despite the fact that they were already seriously considering a separation. She herself had vivid memories of the pain and anxiety her two closest girlhood friends had suffered because their parents tried to hide from the girls the fact that they hated each other. "I always swore," she told me, "that if it happened to me, my kids would be better off if we just told them the truth." Her husband wasn't so sure.

Seeing their parents in ongoing, unresolved bitter quarrels is traumatic for children, but you need to understand that despite all your efforts to put on a show, you won't be able to sweep all the problems under the carpet, and your children will know that you aren't getting along. Even if your fights don't deteriorate into brawls, your children will notice your terse exchanges, your lack of warmth toward each other, the differences between the loving way you talk to them and the tone you use with each other. Of course, keep in mind that if your marital problems have been on-going throughout your children's young lives, they may just see your discord as the way all Moms and Dads behave toward each other. It may not be ideal, but because it's the only life they've known, they may not see it as a new threat to their own security.

Still, there is something to be said for at least a temporary best-foot-forward approach, especially if you are working on resolving your problems. The kids may surmise that something is awry, but you can reassure them that not everything is changing in their home life, at least not yet, and that some things between you won't ever change. Certain routines, such as Saturday family afternoons at the movies and then out for pizza, for example, should be preserved. The rituals around holidays should stay the same, too. Children can learn much from your efforts to remain optimistic through these times. What your children will see is that despite serious problems their parents continue to focus on trying to preserve the good, instead of harping only on the bad. This approach is especially useful when the conflict is one in which children suspect that they will soon have to rely on their parents' goodwill to preserve for them whatever can be maintained of their old life.

You should not feel guilty that you're being dishonest, either, if you hide some aspects of your ongoing marital battles from your children, because they shouldn't be privy to every detail of your disagreement with your spouse. In any serious argument between partners, there is always information that's not appropriate for sharing with children, and it's not hypocritical, but prudent and considerate, to protect them from information at a level of detail they're simply not capable of handling.

Let's look now at how children in various age groups view their parents' marriage crises.

The Child's-Eye View

We spend a great deal of time when children are small helping them learn how to get along with others. A child has a fight with her brother or her friend, and we encourage her to apologize and make up. As all parents know, kids seem to have dozens of fights a day, but recover and go on, often playing happily with their former antagonist within minutes after the two were trying to tear each other apart.

The idea that their parents can have the kind of disagreement that does not lead to a settlement is puzzling and troubling to children. This is especially true because of their special regard for parents as a single, indivisible unit.

Explaining serious parental discord or a divorce to the different age groups requires an understanding of the concerns most likely to surface at each developmental stage. Let's look at our three age groups.

Toddlers

One father I know said that when he and his wife were having a serious crisis in their marriage, their recently toilet-trained two-year-old suddenly lost control wherever he went. No rug was safe. This behavior reflects how a toddler, who can't put his anxiety into words, might react to his parents' battles. He clearly doesn't have the worries of an older child, because he's as yet incapable of understanding how his life may be changed down the road. He only knows that the two most important people in his life are now distracted and are no longer paying him much attention. He can't berate them, so he expresses his anger and anxiety by regressing to a less mature state of being, to a time when he recalls receiving much more attention from them than he's getting now. And it works! When he soils a new rug, his parents pay attention to him. But when this boy's father sat down with him and gently explained that both his parents still loved and cared for him, and once the parents resumed old patterns of attention toward him, his bladder and bowel control vastly improved.

In a situation where a parent is going to be leaving the home as a consequence of a separation or divorce, a toddler must be told the news in the context of his everyday activities, which is what he's most concerned about at this stage. You might say, "Daddy won't be here to make your cereal every day" or "Mommy won't be here to read you a bedtime story or help you brush your teeth." However, you should point out that the parent will do those things at another location and in new time patterns.

A toddler will miss his absent parent, especially if the one leaving has been the primary parent. In any departure, he's bound to show some sadness or act out in various ways. He might not talk much yet, but his reaction will show you that he notices the change. A recently toilet-trained child might regress. A good sleeper might begin waking up at 3:00 a.m.

An older toddler, who is talking more, may continually ask where Daddy or Mommy is, and when he or she is coming over to visit. Some parents, in an effort to protect a very young child, will lie and say that Daddy is away working. Such untruths are never a good idea. The child will soon begin to wonder why his father likes the people at work more than he likes her.

In time, a toddler is more likely than an older child to accept the new family arrangement, since her experience with the old routine was limited. She can soon get used to having Mom through the week and Dad on the weekends, for example. A preschooler or school-age child, on the other hand, will have more difficulty. "My younger son barely questions the way our lives are set up, whereas my older daughter still wonders and has questions about why her father and I don't get along," says one divorced mother of a toddler and a preschooler. What the older child is really asking is why things can't return to the old way she remembers.

Preschool-Age Children
A preschooler will be more troubled than a toddler when she witnesses serious battles between her parents. Because this is the time in their development when many kids develop a crush on the opposite-sex parent, a preschooler may even feel guilty that she played a role in parental arguments. A child can feel jealous of her same-sex parent and secretly wish that she weren't around. Then, when her parents fight, she may feel that her wishes may come true and even that her rival may go away at some time in the future. There is an enormous potential for guilt here, especially if the relationship between the parents continues to deteriorate.

Moreover, once the separation does occur, such a child may feel that now that he's gotten rid of his rival, he has a responsibility to fill his shoes, an awfully big responsibility for a small child.

You have to be very careful to explain to a preschooler that nothing he did caused your divorce to occur. In addition, you must be careful not to let a preschooler reap the spoils of your spouse's parting. A concerned parent might be tempted to allow a preschooler whose sleep has been disturbed to get into bed with her, for example. But it's not a good idea, since it might increase the child's guilt that it was his successful wish fulfillment that brought about the breakup.

A preschooler can comprehend better than a toddler the change that a divorce brings to her home life. Especially if a preschooler goes to nursery school, she may have a wider, fuller circle of friends, and this, combined with her increased maturity, allows her a clearer understanding of two people living in separate places and not being married anymore. The new setup and visiting schedule might need to be explained over and over again because of her reluctance to accept the split, but she probably knows that it exists in the lives of other children.

Young School-Age Children

When a young school-age child sees his parents involved in never-ending fights, he will probably be more embarrassed than a younger child because he now has a social world of his own, in which he must maintain his standing. As far as he can see, his friends' parents don't behave the way his parents do. Yet because he knows at least a few kids whose parents are living apart, or has seen TV shows on the subject, he is also more likely than a preschooler to worry about the possibility of divorce. In fact, a school-age child may know your marriage is on the rocks before you're willing to acknowledge it. "My eight-year-old daughter once asked me at the dinner table—long before divorce was discussed—whether I would be going to an apartment or a condominium when I moved out," said one father who had been surprised by what his daughter had figured out for herself. Because the school-age child now has all these new possibilities in his parents' lives to contemplate, he may not be able to concentrate in school, and his grades may suffer. He may also begin suffering psychosomatic illnesses, such as stomachaches and headaches with no discernible cause other than stress.

If a divorce does occur, a school-age child will spend time brooding about her parents' decision to divorce and may express some self-pity. "How could they do this to me?" is a common refrain. Or: "This isn't fair." Young school-age children tend to be practical and pragmatic, analyzing the effect of a divorce on their own lives, rather than looking at the big picture of Mom and Dad and their relation to each other. One father recalled riding in the car with his seven-year-old son, who suddenly said morosely, "Heather is lucky, she has a car phone and her Dad lives at home."

Since social standing and conforming at school are so important at this age, a school-age child may feel upset at appearing to be different from his friends, many of whom seem to be living with both parents. This idea of fitting within the norm persists despite the higher numbers of divorced people your child knows and the very much reduced number of stereotypical "Leave It to Beaver" families on television and in books.

A school-age child is likely to be more articulate in his anger toward you for breaking up his life and routine. He is also better equipped to play upon your guilt and may become more manipulative in getting things from both parents. Yet there is another side to the coin. Because of his increased social network, the school-age child may have an advantage in dealing with his fears and concerns. Friends, teachers, and counselors can all help by hearing him out on what's troubling him, especially if he's reluctant to discuss the subject with a parent.

Missteps Parents Make

Parent missteps are almost inevitable during crisis periods in marriages, and also during the divorce process and afterward. Marriages don't break up on coldly rational grounds, but because of hurt, anger, frustration, bitter disappointment, heartache, and heartbreak. It is difficult at this time to consistently behave wisely whenever an issue affecting your child arises. As one woman told me, "I was trying to deal rationally with my kids while in the throes of this intense emotional turmoil. It was almost impossible to sit back and reflect on everything I was about to say to them. They'd ask me questions and I'd just react."

Seldom elsewhere in life are you asked to display such mature judgment and discretion at just those times when you feel most like standing up and screaming out your anger or going into your room, throwing yourself on your bed, and crying. Yet these are our children we are talking about, and so we must try.

Here are some common mistakes parents make when talking about serious marital crises or divorce in front of their children.

• *Forcing your child to take sides.* Because of how badly you have been hurt, tearing down your spouse comes naturally as you go through the throes of a marital battle or a divorce. But save the spleen venting for a friend or a therapist. The target of your anger is still your child's other parent, someone your child loves and should continue loving. Furthermore, at such a shaky time your child needs to feel confident that his other parent loves him and can be depended on, even if you feel your spouse has proved to you that he can't be. If you force your child to decide between you and his other parent, he'll be left feeling guilty and filled with doubt, perhaps for the rest of his life. Besides, this strategy can backfire. One woman I know recalled ranting about her husband in front of her daughter, who suddenly burst out, "You don't understand him at all! He's my dad!"

• *Using your child as a confidant.* The period surrounding a divorce or a bitter marital fight can be a lonely one, and it's tempting to confide in your children, who are often eager to help you in whatever way they can. But many of the troubling details of such moments, such as financial matters, a spouse's extramarital affairs, and other heavy topics, must remain off-limits when it comes to talking to your kids. There is nothing wrong with being honest with your child about your feelings of sadness or your anger over the fight or the divorce. But don't overwhelm her with the details. If you do, you are asking her to shoulder a burden of responsibility for your emotional well-being that a child should not have to carry.

• *Using your child as a pawn in the fight against your spouse.* A father I know told his children that he would stop seeing them if their mother did not agree to amend the custody agreement. The children begged their mother to relent, because they truly feared that their father would make good on his threat. In this case, their mother stood firm and the couple was able to work out a plan whereby the father could keep on seeing them.

A mother tells her daughter that their father doesn't care enough about her to want to see her. Only as an adult does the daughter learn that her father was prevented from seeing her by her mother. She now adds to the anger she has long felt toward her father a new anger at her mother.

It is inevitable that manipulating children in this way to

get back at a spouse will ultimately hurt the children. If you tell a child that one of her own parents doesn't care for her, the only reasonable conclusion for the child to come to is that there is something unlovable about her, leaving her with feelings about herself that can haunt her throughout her adult life. Though children can be powerful weapons in a divorce proceeding, using them to advance your own rights or interests is unfair and threatens their emotional health in serious ways. They should not be involved in your battles.

• *Using your child as an intermediary between you and your spouse.* Barbara, an eight-year-old, seemed to be adjusting well to her parents' divorce, when she suddenly began crying again and showing signs of stress at school. What had changed was that Barbara's parents, who despised talking to each other, decided that she was now old enough to convey information between them. The strain of this responsibility started to tell on Barbara, and the effects were as predictable as they were unfortunate for Barbara.

It's easy to begin saying to your children things like "I don't know how your father expects us to live on the measly few dollars he sends us." Even worse may be lines such as the following: "If you need that money for Scouts (or for a new dress), go ask your father."

Children shouldn't be placed in that position. Nor should they be responsible for arranging their weekend visitation schedules or nailing down vacation plans with a noncustodial parent. They are troubled and puzzled enough by their parents' inability to solve their problems. When parents cannot even discuss between themselves the basic arrangements of the new reality, children often feel pressure to take on some of these adult responsibilities before their parents mess things up again. It's never appropriate, at any age, to exploit a child this way.

• *Lying about a separation.* Some parents may believe that they can spare their children the anxiety or pain of a separation by lying about why the absent parent is away: "Daddy is on business in Europe for six months, but he'll be home for Christmas" or "Mommy had to stay with Grandma because she is sick, but she'll come home every weekend." It is vital that you tell children the truth about the absent parent. If your marriage has been under so much strain that you are separating, your children have probably been anticipating this possibility for a while. You might say, "As you probably know, we have been having trouble getting along, so we've decided to live apart for a while."

New Moves

Though it may not seem so while you're still in the thick of it, your getting out of a bad marriage can have positive effects on your children. "When my wife and I finally divorced, our children got us both back again," one father told me. "The arguments, tears, and fights were over at last. Instead of our energies being directed at combating each other, we focused on the kids again. Now, emotionally, I'm with them, and so is their mother."

Because of a bad marriage, this father had worked long hours to avoid the conflict his arrival home always provoked. These days, whenever he is scheduled to have the kids with him, he never brings work home. "I see you more now than when you lived at home," one of his children told him recently.

With the emotional minefield cleared, your kids may

come to know a side of you they had long missed out on. Recently, a divorced father took his children for a daylong outing to an amusement park. At the end of the day, his daughter smiled up at him with great happiness and said, "Dad, I've never seen you laugh so much!"

Getting from those lowest moments back to a full life with your children requires a thoughtful approach about what you say in front of the children along the way and how you say it. Here are the new moves that may help you.

• *New Move 1: Acknowledge that your marriage is in crisis.* Parents often ask me whether they should bring up serious marital problems in front of their children. They wonder if it will make their children anxious and worry them needlessly. This concern becomes particularly pressing when a crisis is escalating.

You should sit down with your children and let them know that something is wrong. If you have a plan you and your spouse are working on, let them in on what you're trying to do to bring it about. You wouldn't, of course, explain all the gory details going on behind the scenes or go into an unending litany of those faults and transgressions on the part of your spouse that led the family to its present dire straits. Remember always that your spouse is your child's other parent and that one of your more important goals through this period is keeping intact your child's relationship with both parents. Instead, you might say, "You've probably noticed that Mommy and I haven't been as friendly toward one another as we used to be. You might be worried about what's going to happen to us." Then let them know exactly what the future holds. "Daddy and I are going to talk to our pastor" or "Mommy and I are going to talk to a marriage counselor who will try to help us solve our problems. Maybe another adult can help us understand what is causing the trouble in our relationship."

Don't be surprised if your children ask exactly what you believe is the trouble in your relationship. Though they may have witnessed fights and arguing, it's the noise and conflict they remember and not the content of the disagreements. When explaining what's wrong, use concrete examples, such as "Daddy and I argue because he spends all his time boating." Or: "Mommy and I both work a lot and we never see each other." Then explain that you both plan to talk about why you do these things, and what you could both do to improve the situation. "Daddy might go out on his boat a little less, and we'll all spend time together as a family, and I'll stop nagging him to sell his boat" could be one example. Sometimes the concrete examples are about surface problems, or symptoms of deeper dissatisfactions. So you could also relate some information such as "We haven't been very thoughtful or considerate toward each other. We're going to try to do something about that."

When talking about faults in your spouse, begin your comments with "I feel . . ." rather than making absolute statements that may be heard as an attempt to turn your child against the other parent. The last thing you want to do at this point is force a child to take sides in a family battle. "I feel" statements show children how you yourself see the situation, without forcing them to agree with your position. "I feel that Daddy doesn't appreciate the way I run things around the house." Or: "I feel that Mommy isn't as happy with me as she used to be."

It's usually at this point in the discussion that children might ask, "What if talking about it doesn't work? What if you and Mommy can't stop arguing?" If the child is asking the question, he or she is already worried about the possibility, so you have an obligation to address the fear. You can explain that while you and your spouse are doing all you can to avoid a breakup, it might occur. Once the possibility of divorce is raised, you should offer all the reassurances to your children that follow.

• *New Move 2: If you are separating, try to put some time frame on the separation.* This may help your children deal with the ambiguity involved in all separations. They certainly will worry about whether you're going to live together again, and at this point you probably cannot give them a black-and-white answer. But if you can say, "In six months, Daddy and I will have a meeting to decide if we can live together again," that may help them focus on that future date. Relate the time frame to a preschooler's activities and the seasons, because her understanding of the passage of time is still shaky. You might say, "After Halloween and Thanksgiving and Christmas, Daddy and I will decide." But expect questions all along during a separation, because your children are likely to keep wondering how you feel and what the decision is likely to be.

• *New Move 3: Tell your children again and again that your marital problems are not their fault.* I cannot overemphasize how important it is to tell children in no uncertain terms that they were not the cause of your marital problems. Studies have shown that some of the biggest problems kids have in coping with their parents' divorce are related to a belief that they played a role in causing it to occur. A child might think: "If only I hadn't fooled around so much or been so bad . . ." Some children, because the fighting and tension between their parents is so stressful, secretly wish that their parents will split up. If they do, a child may then feel guilty that he somehow caused his terrible fantasy to come true.

If you are divorcing, you might say, "Daddy and I (or Mommy and I) do not get along well anymore. Although we loved each other when we got married—and we certainly love having you as our child—we don't love each other anymore. It has nothing to do with you, and it wasn't anything that you did to cause us to feel this way." You should also reassure your toddler or preschooler that you would not divorce them, because children in these age groups may fear that possibility.

A preschooler might reason that after her parents had a fight, one moved out. What happens if she fights with one of them? Will that parent throw her out, or move out on her, too? Parents assume that their children understand the difference between adult loving relationships and parent-child relationships. Sometimes they do and sometimes they don't. Don't take a chance with your children.

• *New Move 4: Explain how life will change for your children when one parent leaves the home.* Your children need to know how a divorce or separation will affect their lives. First and foremost, divorcing parents will have to help children understand that their parents won't live together again. This is the area where you do need to be honest about the concrete facts, even if they are difficult to talk about. The five-year-old daughter of one divorcing father asked him whether he would ever live at home again. Because, in his case, he believed the marriage was utterly over, he was honest and told her the truth, which was no. Some parents think this much honesty is cruel for such a young child, but her question suggests that she is already wondering and worrying about the possibility, so it is better not to leave her to hope in vain and have to suffer the same disappointment again later on.

Be prepared for children to ask you over and over about whether you'll get back together again. This fantasy is powerful and enduring. Even into adulthood, some children of divorce cling to the idea that maybe, someday, somehow, things will work out between their parents. Sometimes even after parents remarry, the fantasy continues and a parent will have to gently remind a child that the relationship between her parents is completely over. Tell them, "We've made new lives now and we won't get married again."

After you've been so honest, you must make sure your child understands that you will most certainly be a part of her life (or reassure her that your departing spouse will be). Give her all the specific details, such as "We will be together every other weekend and you'll stay over with me one day each week." Preschoolers may need simpler explanations, tied to their daily activities, such as "After you go to preschool for five days, Daddy will pick you up and take you to his apartment, where you'll stay with him all weekend. Then, the night before school starts again for the week, Daddy will bring you home." Kids also worry about where their departing parent will go. The parent who is moving out should tell the child exactly where his or her new home or apartment will be. Take your children there and show it to them as soon as possible, so they can get a clear picture of where you will be. Children of all ages wonder how their role in the family will change now that they will be seeing only one parent at a time. Girls need to be reassured that they don't have to play Mommy for Dad. Boys need to know that they don't suddenly have to wear the pants in the family now that Dad has left. Children's psychological roles should not change. They will still be the children in the family. You need to explain that thoroughly.

Of course, other things may change. Children may have to take on more chores if Mom goes back to work outside the home, for example. Or they may be in a day-care setting or after-school program for the same reason. All of these changes may come as a great shock to your children, who naturally cling to their routines for security. Not only have they lost their Dad, for example, but now Mom won't be home after school anymore. Or they may have to spend the whole day with a babysitter for the first time. Be forewarned: young children can spend weeks crying or throwing tantrums when such changes take place, even in families where a divorce isn't occurring. But during a divorce, children are feeling insecure about everything, so their responses to any proposed change may be even more intense. Spend as much time as you can preparing your children for what lies ahead for them. Then, plan to spend a lot of time listening to their complaints. You might say, "I realize how difficult this is. You're probably thinking that if Dad and I had just stayed together, you would not have had to do all this. Maybe that's true. And I'm sorry this is such a big inconvenience. But we'll hang in there and make it through. I understand your feelings and you're certainly entitled to feel annoyed and disappointed."

• *New Move 5: Protect your child from the "adults only" details of marital battles and divorce. But be honest if he or she finds out.* Certain issues during a marriage crisis or a divorce, such as a parent's financial indiscretions or adultery, can be crushing blows to young children, and I suggest that you go light on these details. Young children don't have the ability to incorporate such information into their sense of the world they live in. Often they tend to deny such things. Worrying children about whether there will be enough money to live on can increase their already heightened sense of insecurity about the changes in their lives. And the idea that one parent could go out and take up with a new partner is always shocking to children. Sometimes, though, school-age children, with their sharper sense of the details, will find out about these issues despite all your efforts. Once the cat is out of the bag, you should deal with your children's questions directly and honestly.

One eight-year-old girl I know overheard her mother talking about her husband's affair. Another seven-year-old, after meeting her dad's new girlfriend, remembered meeting her on an earlier occasion while her parents were still married. She figured out the rest. You need to confirm a child's perceptions so that she won't wonder or worry. You might say, "Though married people usually stick with each other as girlfriend and boyfriend, as well as being parents, that didn't happen in our case. It's one of the problems that sometimes occur when married people aren't sure if they love each other anymore." You can go on to add that you felt upset or betrayed, and discuss the matter of trust, but avoid vindictiveness. Reassure your child about financial matters, too. Explain that she will still go to school, and you will still have food to eat and a place to live.

• *New Move 6: For your children's sake, be diplomatic about the other parent's accusations.* One of the toughest situations in which to remain calm is when your spouse maligns you in front of your children. Parents often wonder what to say or do in response, especially if they are intent on trying not to tear down the other parent in front of their children. This is difficult, because it can mean asking kids to take your word over their other parent's or to believe that their other parent did something wrong. But kids are impressionable and you may need to defend yourself. You might take a statesmanlike stance and say, "That's the way he (or she) may see the situation, but it doesn't mean it's necessarily that way." Or try to explain how people say things in anger that they would not otherwise have said. "Mommy is very angry right now, and she's saying how she feels about things." Then tell your child what you believe to be the truth, or at least your side of the story. Because this kind of spillover fighting can make children feel insecure or cause them to wonder if they were to blame (they may even be the topic of the argument), you should once again reassure them. You might say, "Your father should not have said what he did. But I don't want you to worry about it. It's between Dad and me. We'll take care of it."

• *New Move 7: Learn to deal constructively with your children's anger and frustration.* Children can react with fury when their world breaks apart during a bitter marital fight or after a divorce. They're going to blame you both for not making it work and for making their lives miserable. This is especially true for school-age children, who have had more experience of the way things used to be and may be embarrassed about the changes being forced on them. One woman told me that two years after her divorce, her school-age children still don't like to go to parties where there are a lot of fathers around. They much prefer "Moms-only" gatherings, where they can feel comfortable that they're like the other kids.

Don't expect your kids to be understanding about your marriage problems or your divorce. They didn't ask for the changes or the unhappiness, and it's a situation that's entirely beyond their control. Your best bet is to empathize with their feelings. The father whose son was unhappy because his friend had a car phone and a dad at home simply said to his son, "You're right. And I understand that it must make you feel bad." He went on to try to point out some of the positives, too. His son now had two houses, where as his friend with the car phone had only one. Several weeks later, he heard his son whisper to a friend who was in the car with them, "Wait until you see my father's apartment, it's awesome!"

Obviously, the road won't always be this smooth, but as one wise parent told me, "I always give my kids lots of openings to complain, and no matter what they say, I remain a receptive audience."

• *New Move 8: Encourage kids to talk about your marriage struggles or your divorce.* Sometimes children react in silence to the news that their parents are separating or divorcing. Though it's a good idea to try to encourage a child to talk about what he's feeling, don't press the issue too much. He may need to think about it for a while before he can talk about it. It may not be prudent to rush a child or try to pry out of him what he's not ready to talk about. After a divorce, some children may feel uncomfortable talking to either of their parents about their feelings. They may feel that doing so will be disloyal to the other parent. Or they may feel that you will not understand. In this case, try to encourage the children's network of adult friends, relatives, and teachers to help if they can. One mother told me, "My daughter just didn't think I'd understand what she was feeling. I grew up in a home where my parents loved each other and stayed together. Luckily her piano teacher was extremely sympathetic. She told her that her own parents had divorced when she was seven. She encouraged my daughter to talk about it whenever she wanted to, because she knew what it was like." Many schools now have "rap" programs of group therapy for the children of divorce. Your school-age child may not want to call attention to herself by attending, but I would encourage the child to give it a try. One mother I know struck a bargain with her daughter to try the group for the first half of the school year. Her daughter did find the group helpful and stayed on.

Don't expect your child to share the details of such sessions with you. One mother whose daughter attended a rap session eagerly asked her daughter what they talked about after the first day. "I can't tell you. It's . . . it's . . . it's that word that means none of your business, Mom," she replied. "Oh, you mean it's confidential," said her chastened mother. Respect your child's need to talk about negative aspects of the divorce to others without feeling guilty about reporting back to you. The thought of your divorce being discussed by others may be painful for you, but if the process can help your child, you should make every effort to cooperate.

• *New Move 9: Introduce new significant others very slowly.* It will take children a long time to fully accept a new person in your life, and you should not attempt to force your children into liking this new person. It may be that your child will never like the new person, because he sees the new relationship as an intrusion on his own relationship with you. Or a child may feel disloyal to his other parent if he warms too quickly to your new partner. "I tell my kids that they don't need to like my new friend. All I want is for them to love me," said one father. Of course, efforts should be made to encourage a positive relationship between your new companion and the kids. In time, they may be willing to accept the relationship.

I would suggest keeping tenuous relationships away from your children. This is especially important during a separation, when you haven't even decided whether or not you'll divorce. During a separation, your children will be hoping that their parents will reunite. Introducing any potential other partner will make them feel even more vulnerable and confused. Be discreet. The same goes for the period directly after a divorce, while your children are growing accustomed to their parents living apart and not loving one another anymore.

When you have settled into a promising relationship, begin to involve your children slowly and gradually. Perhaps you can arrange some afternoons together with your friend. I wouldn't encourage sleep-overs until your friend is truly a permanent fixture in your life.

Divorced parents sometimes wonder what to do if they meet someone with whom they'd like to share living quarters right away. I don't think this is in the best interests of your children, who are already dealing with so much change. But if you do this, be honest about it to your children. They deserve it. You might say, "I know it's hard for you, but we really love each other and we want to be together." Though it's always important to reassure your children that a new relationship won't change your feelings toward them and that you'll continue to love them, it's critical that you keep giving your child this message when you move into a live-in arrangement. This will require a major adjustment for them, so expect some rocky times. Don't be surprised at some initial strain and awkwardness, and perhaps some testing.

In time, as your children get used to the changes a divorce brings, having them see you give and receive affection and work on a new, loving relationship can be good for them. As they get older, it may help them understand that while not all relationships are permanent, they shouldn't allow one failure to deter them from trying to form new loving attachments. And if your new relationship does turn out to be successful, they'll learn as well that all such relationships don't have to end in disappointment and bitterness.

7
Serious Illness and Death

A woman I know told me that when her mother was thrown from a rider mower and sustained serious head injuries, she decided not to tell her five-year-old daughter about the accident. "My daughter was right in the room with me when I got the call about Mother," she explained. "But I kept my face as calm and blank as I could and didn't tell my husband until later, when our daughter was out of earshot. It was touch and go for a while, and I didn't want to worry my daughter, who adores her Mom-Mom."

This mother thought she had done a good job by sparing her daughter from unnecessary pain, so she was quite surprised at what took place two weeks later. One afternoon, her daughter came to her with her Raggedy Ann doll, the doll's head swathed in makeshift bandages. "Raggedy Ann fell and hurt her head," the child told her mother. "Can you look at her and see if she's all better? Or is she dead?" When assured that Raggedy Ann was indeed all better, the little girl looked at her mother with deep concern. "And do you think Mom-Mom is all better, too?" she asked. "Or is she dead?"

Startled, the mother assured her daughter that her Mom-Mom wasn't dead, that she was getting better every day. Suddenly the child began to sob, releasing all the feelings she'd been bottling up, feelings her mother's silence had convinced her were improper to express.

The mother here had made two false assumptions: one, that her daughter was too young to deal with her grandmother's accident, and two, that she would not learn of it if she weren't told directly. Like most children, this little girl has keenly tuned antennae. An overheard word or two of the hushed phone conversation, a sudden change in her mother's normally sunny disposition, the fact that her grandmother had not called or visited for weeks, the grim looks that passed between her parents—all confirmed that something was seriously wrong with her grandmother. Ironically, her mother's efforts to shield her left her to deal with her fears alone.

Few things arouse more anxiety than illness or death, and children will become aware of this new anxiety before a word is addressed to them. Even short-term health problems, such as a broken leg or minor surgery, as well as chronic illnesses such as asthma or diabetes, can cause family stress that a child will read correctly. But as difficult and painful as these problems can be, parents need to find ways to explain them to their children. The reasons they must do so are varied, but all are equally important.

As the mother above learned, there is no hiding such painful information from children, anyway. Despite your best efforts, your children will know something is wrong. Yet, without your help in explaining and interpreting what exactly is wrong, children may magnify or distort the problem, probably making it much more frightening than it actually is. At other times, they will shut off their feelings.

Being able to talk with your children about the illness or death of a loved one will teach them that such topics, though painful, are a part of life, and that they can be discussed openly among people who share the pain and concern. Whether someone you love has a chronic illness or is ill and dying, telling your children how you feel lets them know that feelings of sadness are okay at these times. As you discuss the situation with your children, you will also be teaching them the language of loss, something important for them to know when as adults they will be called on to comfort friends who have sustained a loss.

Do you recall how you felt as a child when the topic was brushed aside or awkwardly dealt with by your parents? One woman who was only a child when her grandmother died recalls that her father simply went about business as usual, despite the fact that his mother had died. It was only when his wife in effect forced him to tell his children about the death that the floodgates opened. He cried inconsolably in his wife's arms in front of the children, then ran out of the house, mortified that they had witnessed it. Another woman recalled that when she asked her mother if her father was dying, her mother said she didn't know, then proceeded to open the phone book, looking in the Yellow Pages under funeral homes.

In both examples, the children learned that death was a topic their parents were utterly incapable of discussing without shame or deception. And it increased the confusion these children felt about the whole subject.

Many parents worry that they won't be able to discuss such painful matters without losing control and crying. And they're concerned that if children see a parent so vulnerable, they'll become frightened themselves. It isn't such a bad thing for your children to see you cry, as long as you assure them that you are not seriously ill yourself and that you are still enough in control to manage your life and theirs. Besides, seeing you cry and then compose yourself again teaches children that great sadness can come into your life, but you can recover and go on.

When illness strikes one of the parents, a whole new set of factors come into the equation. Your first concern may be that if the children learn of it they will be thrown into panic, unnecessarily so if the illness is not life-threatening. But it is inevitable that children will quickly figure out that something's going on, even if they don't zero in on exactly what it is. You might not say much to the children, but suddenly there are medicines everywhere. The ill parent is making weekly trips to the doctor, instead of twice a year. The children are staying with neighbors and friends more often, but no one is telling them why. Grownups they know are talking differently to them, with a mixture of compassion and fear in their eyes. There are whispered discussions nearly every day.

One mother of four, whose husband survived a life-threatening heart condition, said her children witnessed frightening episodes of their father's condition, which made it very real to them. But, she said, "What scared them the most is that they didn't know what was happening and how it would likely end." As a result, she and her husband made the decision to share with them each step in his therapy; as they did, they saw many of their children's fears calmed.

Even if the illness in your house isn't life-threatening, keep in mind that your children don't know that unless you tell them so. Doctors report that a quite common question they get after their diagnosis of any serious illness is "Can this condition be life-threatening?" Children have the same concern about any illness that strikes their parents, though they may not know how to phrase the appropriate question.

A woman I know who had to have her gallbladder removed spent about a week feeling pretty sick before going into the hospital for surgery. Though the recovery would be difficult, especially with two children aged two and five to worry about, she was relieved that the riskiest part, the surgery, was over. Yet her five-year-old came to her as she was recovering and said, "Mom, are you going to die?" She hadn't faced the fact that her frustration at the pain and then her nervousness and anxiety about caring for two small children after surgery would all be noticed by her son, and that he would choose the worst-case scenario to dwell on. She had also forgotten that her children, without straightforward explanations about what was involved, would have no way of knowing that her getting past the surgery safely meant that the worst was behind her.

Unfortunately, if you are dealing with the imminent or recent death of a loved one you must be aware that you may have trouble coming to terms with your own feelings. As you go through some of the common stages of grief, such as denial, anger, and depression, you may find difficulty getting yourself to discuss the facts with your children in ways that will be most helpful to them.

You may have convinced yourself that there is no way to put the facts before your children without hurting them. Yet in the end you have to face that when you say you want to protect your children from having to deal with the painful reality confronting the family, you are still protecting yourself. As long as you don't have to explain it to them, you can keep from dealing with it yourself for a while longer. This is an understandable reaction to such emotionally charged events. But you must also recall that no matter how you try to shield them, children will have anxieties that they—and you—really must deal with. Death often provokes in children a concern about who else might be going to die soon, and high on this list of potential candidates are their parents. It's a frightening thought, and one about which they surely need your reassurance. In trying to deal with this situation, you might also keep in mind that talking with your child can help you gain some insight into your own feelings, and this may help you as well as your child.

This chapter will help you put your feelings into words, and help you to judge exactly what you should and should not tell your children about illness and death.

The Child's-Eye View

Our three different age groups—the toddler, the preschooler, and the young school-age child—all have a slightly different view of serious illnesses and death.

Toddlers

Toddlers cannot really fathom the finality of death or the seriousness of an illness that may lead to death. It's out of their immediate experience. They don't have the maturity yet to focus on any one thing for very long. Even in the gravest of situations, a toddler will still be more concerned with her diaper, her cookie, or climbing up on that high shelf. Besides, a toddler's sense of permanence and her concept of time are not yet fully developed. Toddlers live in a fanciful world: Grandma died, but she may come back. Grandma is really sick, but she could be better tomorrow.

It's also hard for toddlers to empathize with your feelings. A toddler may miss a grandparent for a while, but it won't last, and the feelings of loss will be short-lived unless the grandparent was a regular part of the child's activities. The toddler's world will be turned upside down if he loses a parent or a sibling, however. He's lost someone with whom he interacted on a daily basis.

What a toddler does understand, even concerning the illness or death of someone peripheral to her life (such as a faraway grandparent or uncle), is the emotion of such moments. If Mommy or Daddy is very upset, that's enough to distress her, too. Sometimes, however, children take in more than we realize. June, the mother of a toddler, lost her own brother in a tragic fire. She spent a great deal of time on the phone in the days following the accident, trying to find out if her brother had suffered a great deal and to learn something about the subject of fatal home fires in general. She also inquired about smoke alarms and about whether or not a properly placed smoke alarm might have saved her brother.

At this time, the toddler wasn't old enough to articulate his concern about the incident that had upset his mother so much. But obviously the emotional impact registered deeply, for many months later, when he was more verbal, whenever he visited other people in their homes he demanded to know where their smoke alarms were.

I advised June to talk to her child, to ask him what he remembered of the fire and find out what he was thinking about the uncle who had died. She learned that he was principally concerned about his mother, who had been absent through much of the ordeal and too distracted to deal with him, and that his questions about smoke alarms were his attempts to ensure that another fire would not upset his mother in the same way.

Be aware that a toddler may also pick up on the everyday inconvenience that accompanies even a short-term illness or a chronic condition that poses no real threat. A mother who was recovering from a cesarean operation after the birth of her second child remembered that her two-year-old daughter was distraught and inconsolable because Mommy could no longer pick her up, an unfortunate introduction to the new sibling.

Preschool-Age Children

When children are nearing the age of four, they often begin to ask a lot of questions about death and dying. Over the years, I've talked with hundreds of parents who worried that their preschoolers were becoming overly macabre. My hunch is that it's all part of a package at this age. They're curious about how life begins, so they ask a lot of questions about reproduction; and they're curious about how it all ends, so they ask about death. The questions can be truly painful for parents to answer: "Will you die soon?" "Am I going to die?" "When are we all going to die?" "What happens when we die?"

That preschoolers worry and fret about these questions is an indication of their growth, not something for parents to see as abnormal. Indeed, this might be an appropriate age for you to begin bringing the topic up, even if your children don't. Don't be disappointed, however, to learn that no matter how you present the subject to preschoolers, their first concepts of death will remain childlike. Children of this age can give you comical answers when you question them about their understanding of death. "When you die you get smaller . . . you fall down . . . you fly up in the sky." Yet, when you think about it, their conjectures are as good as ours! Death is a puzzle to all of us, because nobody really knows what it means to be dead. You can give a scientific description of death and impart any hopes or religious beliefs you may have about the survival of the spiritual side of humans, but that's about all. Preschoolers are beginning their lifelong journey toward understanding this difficult topic for themselves.

How will a preschooler react if someone close to her becomes seriously ill or dies? Because of her egocentricity at this age, her own vulnerability may be her first concern. Next is her worry that her parents may die, too. Who will take care of her then? Your child will not likely raise these concerns with you, so if a death or serious illness strikes your family, you should bring the topic up and encourage your child to express his worst fears. Remember to have a discussion on the topic of death even if the illness that strikes is brief or not that serious, because preschoolers are so likely to think "death" even in the most benign situations. A preschooler I know was absolutely certain that his dad was going to die because he spent a week in bed and couldn't play ball with him as he always had before. When there is an illness in the house, something as simple as a parent who doesn't smile as much or who spends more time sleeping in the middle of the day can really worry the routine-oriented preschooler.

School-Age Children

A six-year-old girl I know recently gave this definition of death: "Your body rots, and goes into the ground, but your spirit survives somewhere, like heaven." When asked what "spirit" was, she replied: "It's what makes you taste and feel things." This child was showing that she was at an age where she understood something about intangibles. She was becoming capable of abstract thinking about death and dying. Yet she was also able to understand that when you die your body cannot magically reappear, even if your spirit might survive somewhere.

Because school-age children can talk about death with some understanding, and because they're that much older and emotionally involved with those around them, the news that a beloved relative or friend has died may hit them harder. Yet school-age children may be uncomfortable talking about their feelings, so it may be even more difficult for a parent to figure out how children this age are taking a serious illness or death. One mother told me that when her mother died very suddenly of a heart attack, she expected her two school-age daughters to be distraught. They had spent a great deal of time with their grandmother and had shared many happy times with her. But neither had a thing to say when their mother asked them how they felt about it.

Bringing the topic up was clearly the right thing for the mother to do. It is possible that in this case the children had not been as emotionally attached to their grandmother as their mother believed, for children do vary in how related or emotionally involved they become to others. But it's also possible that these two girls simply didn't know how to respond when their mother asked them how they felt. Perhaps a better way to take the emotional pulse of school-age kids experiencing the death of a close person in their lives is to approach them something like this: "What did you want to do when you heard the news that Grandma had died?"

Because children this age are much more action-oriented, a child may be better able to tell you that she wanted to "ride my bike for fifty miles" or "be alone in my room" than to recall for you what her feelings were at such a difficult moment.

School-age children would rather not stop and be introspective. They don't want to feel bad, so as a coping mechanism they may feign a lack of interest. Learning that someone else is seriously ill or dying may raise a concern with them about whether their own parents are going to die, so you should make it a point to reassure them that you are all right. Although kids this age will have a better understanding of short-term, non-serious illness, you should still explain enough of the details to assure them that a non-life-threatening illness is just that, even though the sick person may look different (perhaps be in a wheelchair or on crutches) or have to spend some time in a hospital.

What if a Child's Parent, Sibling, or Friend Dies?

When a child's parent, sibling, or a close friend dies, important aspects of his emotional life can be thrown into chaos. He may feel a tremendous sense of vulnerability. He thought his parents were strong enough, and in control enough, to protect those he loves from being taken away from him forever. Now he finds out it just wasn't true.

This is especially the case if the person was his primary caregiver. Because of the unique attachment a young child forms to his primary caregiver, the death of this person will strike the child like the loss of a piece of himself. Although a toddler's immediate surface response may be mild, the cumulative effect of all he's feeling may be quite profound as he grows up, and then over the course of his life.

The best way to handle this most tragic situation is to tell the child the truth. As hard as it may be to believe, I've had several people who consulted me on this topic tell me that they planned not to tell the child of her parent's death. In one instance, the child's aunt planned on "taking her mother's place." Another woman told me she planned to say that the child's mother was off on a trip and wouldn't return. A moment's thought about such a course of action would raise troubling questions. What would a child think of a mother who would go off and leave her that way? She'd wonder why Mommy didn't keep in touch, why she was mad, why she had done this to her. She also might be filled with guilt, wondering what she had done to make Mommy so mad that she would go away.

As cruel as this sounds, you must make it clear to the child that death means her parent is not coming back. Well-meaning people trying to protect a child from the real meaning of death don't realize that it would be much worse for a child to imagine her parent living somewhere else and forgetting about her. The sense of rejection and abandonment a child would feel at such news would doubtless affect her ability ever to love or trust anyone again.

With toddlers and preschoolers, you may have to explain the permanence of death again and again, since their concept of "gone forever" is not yet developed. Explain that Mommy or Daddy didn't want to or choose to die, but that the illness or accident caused it to happen.

The evidence suggests that when preschoolers or school-age children lose a primary caregiver, the experience is very often, but not always, the cause of emotional instability later on. Such a negative outcome can be made less likely and less severe if immediately after the primary caregiver's death the child's other caregivers spend a great deal of time helping the child come to terms with this profound loss.

A sibling's death, on the other hand, can bring out feelings of ambivalence in the surviving child. She may have felt anger during the illness because all attention was focused on the sick child. But now that the sibling has died, her anger may turn to enormous guilt that she somehow caused it to happen. Reassure your child that the death wasn't her fault and that her feelings of anger are a natural reaction. A school-age child would be likely to make those connections between her feelings of anger and the resulting death of the object of her anger, because she is old enough to understand some logic, even if her understanding is flawed.

When a sibling or a friend dies, children may sometimes begin to worry that they, too, will die. This is especially true of older preschoolers and school-age kids. The event upsets their prior sense of what death is: something that happens to old people. Be sure to offer reassurance. Tell him, "You're healthy and safe, and we will always take good care of you."

Finally, resist the very natural urge to be overprotective of your surviving child after the death of a sibling or friend. And don't place unreasonable expectations on her that she must fill the shoes of a sibling who died. The morbid sense of duty such parental messages communicate to the surviving child can seriously hamper her emotional development.

Euthanasia:
A Decision Better Kept from Children

Though I advocate honesty on most topics concerning serious illness and death, when it comes to discontinuing life support for a terminally ill person I think it best not to share your decision with your children. These days, there's a lot in the news about the topic, and a national debate is going on about the ethics and legality of various actions and decisions not to act. Some of the brightest minds in our country, including theologians, physicians, professors, philosophers, and ethicists, are grappling with the issue. I don't think we can expect a child to understand why a parent would discontinue life support for a beloved grand-father. Even if you explain that Grandpa is technically not alive anymore, a child may still hold you responsible for killing him. It would be better simply to tell the child that her grandfather died.

The same advice holds for an animal who's euthanized. To your child, an animal can be as dear as any relative or friend. The issues involved are simply too complex, and he doesn't yet have the life experience to weigh the alternatives and remain at peace with the decision.

If an older, school-age child brings up the topic of eu-thanasia because she's seen something about it on TV, however, there would be nothing wrong with discussing it under these less personal circumstances. You might tell your child this: "If a person can't go on living unless he or she is kept alive by machines, that's not really living as we understand it. The person can't talk, or eat, or play games anymore. When that happens, some people say they would prefer that the machines be taken away so they can die naturally." Explain that people sometimes write down this wish or tell their relatives about it. It would also be helpful to explain that in most cases this can't be done unless someone close comes forward and says this is what the person would want for himself or herself in this situation.

Suicide

If a child loses a parent or close relative to suicide, very special precautions need to be taken. The impact of a suicide on a child can be quite severe. Survivors of suicides often feel a combination of guilt, rage, sadness, abandonment, and shame. Another important concern is that children whose parents commit suicide are more likely to consider suicide themselves.

Depending on the circumstances and the age of the child, the fact of a suicide may be very hard to keep from a youngster. If the child is a preschooler when it occurs, revealing that death was by suicide can be postponed for a while. After things have settled down, an explanation is in order. Of course, if a preschooler has overheard the news and has some idea the person took his own life, then it should not be left to the child's imagination to fill in the blank spaces. The older the child, the more complete you will have to be with your explanations.

What you say to your child will depend on the particulars of the situation as well as his age. There are many different motives for suicidal behavior. Despair over losing a loved one, a terminal illness, severe depression, and guilt over an unethical or illegal activity are some of the more common reasons. Determining whether the death was accidental or a suicide can at times be difficult, for some suicidal people engage in risky activities that can result in a death that can seem to be accidental.

You may have mixed feelings about suicide. You may believe that suicide is never justified under any circumstances, or you may believe that there are occasions when it is. Know your own attitude before talking to your child. If it is your spouse who has died, you will naturally be in an emotional state. Wait until you feel that you can manage a relatively calm dialogue with your child.

Before you begin with your child, however, always learn from him what he thinks has taken place. You must always start with what the child knows and then tailor what you tell him to his own level of comprehension. I suggest that you begin by simply asking, "What do you think happened?" After listening to the answer, begin piecing the true story together with the child. For example, after learning that he does know that his mother has died, you might go on this way: "Yes, Mommy was very sick for a long time. Then she got sicker, and the doctors didn't think she would get better." Remember to interrupt your story frequently to ask your child to talk about what you have told him so far, as he understands it.

Gradually, the method of death can be brought up. You can ask, "Do you know how Uncle James died?" You may be surprised to hear how much the child has garnered from the conversations around him. Sometimes children know more than they are prepared to say, but want to hear it from you. "You may have heard some people say that he committed suicide," you can say. "Do you know what that means?" The child may have a tentative notion about it. "It means that the person made himself die" is one way of conveying the idea of suicide to a child. I would not be terribly graphic about the means of suicide. If a person took an overdose of pills, you might say, "He took so many pills that his body got poisoned."

Although it is a topic fraught with emotion, it is a good idea to talk about the many controversies that accompany the subject of suicide. Is it cowardly? Is it courageous? Is it ever justifiable? are the types of questions that can be discussed in an educational way with a school-age child. It is also necessary to acknowledge the child's emotional response to the situation, and to reassure him that his reaction is appropriate. He should know that some combination of horror, grief, anger, and sadness is perfectly understandable. You might say, "It is very hard to think that people would do that to themselves. I am upset about it. I wish he were still alive. It makes me mad to think that he won't be here anymore." As with other serious family matters, it is important to remind children that they were not the cause of what occurred, and that they could not have done anything to prevent it from happening.

I am inclined to recommend counseling for any child whose parent has committed suicide. Because there is so much ambivalence in a surviving child's mind, the mental-health risks are very great. It is perilous to allow a child to harbor unspoken thoughts and feelings that may influence his behavior as an adult. Here is an instance where psychotherapy can be a useful preventive approach.

When Children Respond to Death with Jokes, Anger, or Games

"If Grandpa dies, who'll clean the pool for us?" jokes a six-year-old to her shocked father, who has just told her that his father is gravely ill. "I didn't like Grandma, anyway," says a furious five-year-old when told that the grandmother he loved very much has just died. "She never let me stay up late or watch the TV shows I liked!"

It's just days after you've attended services for your mother. You come upon your six- and eight-year-old children playing dead in the living room. "Hey, are you dead yet?" you hear your son shout to your daughter, who is lying rigid on the floor, surrounded by potted plants. When she shakes her head mischievously, he shouts: "Oh no? Here, *bam! bam!*" and pulls the trigger of an imaginary gun. To a parent still reeling from a recent death, it may seem inconceivable that children can act this way. It's hard not to lose your temper and reprimand your kids harshly for their lack of sensitivity. I've had parents whose children behaved this way tell me that they screamed, "You're terrible for doing that!" or "Don't play that way!" right in their children's surprised faces. Such a harsh reprimand tells your children that they've stumbled onto a completely taboo subject. They may react by never raising with you their questions, fears, and anxieties about death.

The reason you must make the effort to remain calm is that joking, playing, or getting angry are prime methods children use to take control of their apprehensions about death or to release strongly felt emotions. And children aren't the only ones who do it, by the way. Why is it that almost immediately after the tragic deaths of famous people, jokes about them begin to circulate? What about the anger adults often feel toward a helplessly ill relative for whom they have to care? Such feelings do exist, and we cannot expect children to hide them better than adults do.

The child who was joking to her father about her grandfather cleaning the pool was using humor to try to make concrete sense out of a grim situation. Children don't think of their behavior as being irreverent, and you must accept that it's really okay for them to do it. As long as they don't embarrass anyone or hurt someone's feelings, such humor releases the tension they are feeling all around them.

Playing dead—or pretend killing—is another tension releaser, though here kids are attempting to overcome their own feelings of vulnerability. School-age children especially may not be able to put their fears about death into words.

Instead, they show by their actions how they feel. Games such as the one described above, where they've taken control of death and decided on what terms and when it will occur, make them feel like active participants instead of passive victims.

Though preschoolers are more likely to ask you directly about death, they, too, play war games and kill each other in pretend play, an outlet for all the ruminating they do about death at that age. These represent effective ways for children of this age to deal with and develop some control over their fear. Don't look for too much consistency here. They worry about death, yet cheer when a cartoon superhero pulverizes some villain.

There's nothing wrong with your pointing out that there are fantasy deaths and real deaths, but your child will probably go on playing dead to explore his own feelings on the topic. If you're concerned that your child may not completely understand the finality or reality of death because of all the time he spends in pretend killing, you can look for a death in nature to provide an opportunity to show him the difference. Whether it's a dead bird, an animal on the road, or a picture of some animals with their prey in a nature magazine, point out what real death means.

Interpret your children's jokes about death and dying, or their playing killing games, as signals that they're trying to work out their fears. You have to learn to read this behavior. Then try to discuss with them the fears they are trying to deal with so obliquely. You might say, "You must be puzzled about what it is like to die." Their responses may help you understand what they're feeling and lessen your anger about the way they have expressed it.

Parents should also understand that anger is another way of dealing with strong emotions, even among children. Disavowing someone beloved who has died expresses how strongly hurt a child feels about being abandoned. You should acknowledge your child's strong feelings at such a moment and reassure her that it's okay to feel this anger, for a child can feel guilty about anger toward a dying or deceased person, just as an adult can. You might say to your child, "I know that you're mad at Grandma for dying. You feel she left you. You also feel sad because you miss her. Sometimes when you get sad, it makes you angry at the person who caused the sadness, even if it wasn't her fault. But you can't help feeling angry. And it's okay to have those feelings."

Missteps Parents Make

When considering how to approach your children concerning the serious illness or death of someone to whom they—and you—are very close, you should begin by giving yourself a break and not judging yourself too harshly. Chances are this is a very stressful time for you, too. At times when you are under this level of stress it's hard not to react inappropriately to things your children do or say. Nevertheless, your children do need you to respond to their concerns and fears.

What follows is a brief list of the undesirable ways of dealing with illness and death, ways you may be repeating simply because that's the way your parents dealt with you through these kinds of experiences. Following this list, I'll suggest "New Moves" to help you approach your children's concerns constructively.

• *Lying about or hiding a death or serious illness.* You should avoid statements such as "Everything will be all right." It's a pat answer and a patronizing one. To a child, saying everything will be all right means that it will return to what it was, something certainly not always true in these kinds of situations. Such statements don't prepare children for the possibility that the worst may occur, which they will fear, anyway. What is important to them is their belief that they can rely on you to guide and protect them through the difficult times, a belief that will be undercut if they suspect you are not telling them the truth. I've already discussed how futile trying to hide a serious illness or death from children can be; it doesn't work most of the time, because children are incredibly good at figuring things out. And it's almost as bad if it does work. What possible explanation could you give a child for the disappearance of someone he thought loved him? His hurt and sense of betrayal will be more harmful to him than if you'd told him the truth to begin with.

Don't hide from your children the truth about your family's past history of deaths, troubling illnesses, and disabilities. Many families try to cover up, or just avoid talking about these things. A man I know remembered that as a teenager he had seen a baby in a crib who had something obviously wrong with her. His family brushed it off, telling him the baby had the flu or some other childhood illness. Now he realizes that the baby was probably disabled, that his parents just couldn't bring themselves to talk about so unpleasant a reality.

You should explain the family's history of both mental and physical illnesses to your children. Don't keep secret a child who died before your present children were born, either. Your children may stumble upon evidence of this other child and wonder why you didn't tell them and what else you might be hiding.

• *Distorting death.* To describe death as being like sleeping, for example, is almost a guarantee of nightmares. Kids already find it "yucky" to imagine a body buried under the earth. What could a child possibly think if you tell her the person is asleep? Besides, you may have a great deal of difficulty getting her to go to sleep from then on, when she realizes that her poor grandfather took a nap and to this day hasn't awakened from it.

• *Admonishing kids for asking questions about death.* A child asks, "Will Grandpa die?" His parents respond, "How could you say that! We're hoping that Grandpa will live!" If you haven't yet squarely faced the possibility that one of your own parents, or someone else you love, may die, a child's direct question can be very painful. But the question is innocent: a child isn't aware yet that death is a subject around which we all tiptoe. Your responding with anger teaches your child that the topic is not open for discussion. That leaves her with her own fears and with no one to turn to for answers to her questions.

• *Talking in hushed tones without explanation.* Rebecca recalled a time in her own childhood when her sister became very ill and went to the hospital suddenly with her parents. When her parents came home, Rebecca could see that her mother had been crying. Then her parents stood nearby, talking in hushed tones to the babysitter, shooing Rebecca away when she came near. What was wrong with her sister? Was she dead? Would she ever come home again? Later, Rebecca learned that her sister was going to be okay, but she spent agonizing hours speculating hopelessly about what had happened. When children witness hushed tones and other such worrisome behavior in their parents, they are owed some explanation of what's going on. Otherwise, you've left them with nothing but their fears.

- *Minimizing the death of a pet.* A woman I know remembered that as a child she wanted to have a funeral for her dog which had died. Her parents refused, saying that a dog's death didn't warrant it. She still remembers how hurt and shocked she was that her parents so belittled her deep feelings toward her dog. By all means you should take a pet's death seriously when your child does, and be respectful of his sadness at such a time. Have a memorial service or plant a flower in honor of the animal. Have a good cry with your child and reminisce about the pet. All this will confirm for him that it's proper to care about all living creatures.

- *Excluding children from funerals and memorial services.* Children need to put closure on death, just as adults do. A parent called me recently to say that his father had died. He was wondering whether he should take his kids out of their summer camp and bring them home for the funeral. There was a games competition going on and he didn't want them to miss it. He was thoroughly conflicted. I told him that he should go get them, bring them home, let them attend services, then take them right back to camp. To do otherwise would rob them of the chance to say goodbye to their grandfather. The children would feel that their father had minimized their importance, that he had not respected them enough to include them in this ritual in which so many other family members participated. When death occurs, there must be a conclusion for children, too. Many people assume kids don't need it, but they do.

The kids responded well and the interruption did not ruin their summer, as their father had feared it would.

New Moves

Because of our own anxieties and ambivalence about death and illness, we may feel at a loss in trying to handle our children's curiosity, questions, and fears. Here are some New Moves to help you deal with these topics in ways that employ the maturity, wisdom, and sense that your children deserve from you.

• *New Move 1: Help your child learn to cope with the disruptions at home that accompany illness.* If someone in your home is seriously or chronically ill, your children may have difficulty adjusting to the changes required of them. For example, having to be quiet all the time is a hardship on normally boisterous kids. But you cannot make a bad situation good, so the best you can do is to try not to lose your temper and keep reminding them of the new rules. Acknowledge how unfair it must seem to them, but explain that you don't have an option. And help them find alternatives when possible, such as allowing them to play outside or arranging for them to play at friends' houses.

Some parents worry that they shouldn't expose kids to some of the so-called scary parts of caring for an ill person, such as the medicines and medical equipment. But one mother whose husband was seriously ill said her children quickly adapted to the new reality. "Kids take their cue from you. If you make it part of the new routine of the house and you carry on with the family's life, they'll accept it readily," she said. "The presence of a lot of medicine just became a part of their lives." You may have to explain the function and purpose of the medication and equipment to demystify it all. Children should be encouraged to express their irritation with any part of the new arrangement that bothers them.

• *New Move 2: Talk to your kids about good things ahead.* Even with short-term illnesses, or non-life-threatening chronic illnesses, the mood around your house can become pretty somber and discouraging. You should remind your children that it won't be this way forever. You might remind the children of an ill grandparent, "As soon as Grandma is on her feet again, she'll be coming for dinner again on Sundays." Or if someone has been confined to a wheelchair and is having trouble adapting to it, remind your children that some things will get easier. You might tell them, for example, "Once Dad learns how to get in and out of the car and negotiate ramps, we'll be able to go to the mall again." As adults, we have had life's experience to teach us that bad things get better, or we finally adapt ourselves to them better, but children do not. They may truly think it's going to be sad and grim around the place forever.

At the same time, of course, there will be less in the way of physical activity with a parent who is confined to a wheelchair. This will be experienced as a deprivation, especially if that parent was formerly active with the children. Expect some arguments, tantrums, and whining coming out of the change, whether or not the children connect their upset state to the change.

• *New Move 3: Explain matter-of-factly what death is.* Your children need to learn that death is a part of life. Everyone dies. Tell your children honestly what happens to bring about death, that the heart stops beating, the brain stops functioning, and the person stops breathing. Explain that the deceased won't be able to talk or walk around anymore and that he or she never will again. Be honest as well about what is done to bodies after people die, that they are buried or cremated.

If you've had a miscarriage or a stillborn child, be sure to explain those deaths, too, because they are very real to children. When explaining miscarriage, you can say, "The baby wasn't ready to be born. It didn't have all the parts it needed to live." You could link it to a discussion about the body and how people need the heart, brain, lungs, and other organs to live.

• *New Move 4: Reassure your child that you and he are all right.* Unless of course it's a parent who is seriously ill or who has died, you should reassure the child who asks, "Will I die? . . . Are you going to die? . . . When will you die?" that you are not sick and not old enough to die. As a matter of fact, you should do this whether your child asks or not, since all children worry about these issues when someone close to them gets very ill or dies. Sometimes they worry about it without immediate cause. One six-year-old I know asked his mother repeatedly to tell him how old she was when her own mother died. She was nineteen years old at the time. She could almost see him adding up in his head how many years he had left before he had to start worrying about losing his own mother.

It's hard, of course, to tell your child that someday you, too, will die. You might try what one mother told her preschooler, to convince him that her death wasn't something he had to worry about in the present. She said: "First you'll go to nursery school, then there's kindergarten and first grade and second grade, and you'll go to camp, then you'll be a teenager, and you'll go to college, and get a job and get married and have children of your own . . ." And on it went, until her son was convinced that an awful lot was

going to happen between now and the awful "then" he was
worrying about.

Even though you can give them no guarantee, small
children need to have the belief reinforced that you're not
in any danger of leaving them. "I'm not dying, and I plan
to be around for a long, long time."

• *New Move 5: Create opportunities to talk about death in general.*
Before the topic is forced onto your family, practice talking
about death and what it means. Use an opportunity such
as the death of an old baseball player or a local celebrity.
The same holds true for aged distant relatives who have
died. It's a lot easier to explain the basics about death when
you're talking about someone in whom you and your child
have no deep emotional investment.

• *New Move 6: Allow children who attend funerals to ask questions openly.* A mother I know took her five-year-old daughter to the funeral of an aunt whom the daughter had known.
Even at that age, her daughter understood the solemnity
of the event and sat quietly through the prayers and eu-
logies. She asked lots of practical questions, too. There was
an open casket, and many of her questions reflected a curiosity about what happens to the body after death. "Why
is her hair dyed a different color? Why does her skin look
so different from a live person's? Her face is puffy, why?
She can't wake up, can she, even though she looks asleep?"
The little girl saw some other relatives cry, and she heard
a lot of fond memories about her aunt recalled by others.
She even remembered herself that the woman had given
her a big white stuffed bear once, and that her aunt had
enjoyed listening to Christmas carols when she spent the
last holiday with the little girl and her parents. Such meth-

ods by which we say goodbye to a person who has died are as important for children as for adults.

Some parents worry about whether to let their children see embalmed bodies. Much of your decision should depend on your family's tradition and customs. One woman I know remembered that when she was growing up all of her family's funerals were held at home. She saw many a dead body right in the living room. It didn't worry her in the least. That was just what her family did after a death. If open caskets are a matter of course in your family, your child will come to accept them. Of course, you should consider the personalities of your own children and shield them if you think seeing any part of the ritual will upset them a great deal. Though children should learn that a dead person need not be feared, they should not be pressed to view the body.

• *New Move 7: Prepare children for a possible death, but explain the concept of hope.* Children need to begin the tentative process of separation from a person who may be dying, so parents need to prepare them by telling them exactly how ill the person is. You might say, "I know you've noticed that we've been very worried and have spent a lot of time on the phone talking to the doctor lately. I wanted you to know that we're okay, but your grandpa is very ill. The doctor is doing everything he can to help him." If your child asks whether the person will die, be honest. In the majority of cases, you can say that you just don't know for sure. With the strides being made in medicine today, that is more often than not the most accurate statement you can make. You might add: "Grandpa could die, but he might not. The medicine he's taking is very powerful and the doctor says the odds are good." If you know that the chances are slim, don't hesitate to tell your children so, but add that there's always hope, and if such is the custom in your family, prayer. Add, "I'll let you know as soon as we learn new things about how Grandpa is doing." Including your child this way shows her that you respect her as an important member of the family, and if the situation is grave, you've begun to prepare her for the possibility of death. Keep checking in with your child as the illness continues, to see how she's feeling and to find out what new concerns she may have. And keep your promise to apprise her of the patient's condition, so that she knows that she can rest easy unless you tell her otherwise, and so she will not be surprised by the outcome if the worst does occur.

Be sure to distinguish between serious, life-threatening illnesses and common sicknesses that children have. They may begin to fear getting sick because they may think that all sickness can lead to death. A father I know was surprised when his children asked if their uncle's cancer was contagious. Then he realized that his children were probably thinking about the little sicknesses they get, most of which they have been told are very contagious.

• *New Move 8: Explain to your children how sad you feel when someone you love is dying.* Ethan's father was dying of lung cancer, yet he had avoided saying anything at all to his children beyond the basic fact that his father was sick. The children noticed that he was tense, irritable, and much harder to live with. Yet he couldn't bring himself to share with them all the complicated, conflicted feelings he had.

I told Ethan it was very important that he reveal his feelings to his children. Parents can help children find the words to express sadness when they learn to voice those feelings themselves. I reassured him that even if he broke down and cried no damage would be done to his kids or the relationship between him and them. Rather, they would learn that their dad has a whole range of emotions they didn't know he had.

It's always helpful for children to learn how their parents tolerate uncomfortable feelings, so that they can eventually adopt those ways themselves. Your children may become upset when you cry, but as long as you reassure them that you are all right and not going to leave them, you can explain that you're feeling sad.

I advised Ethan to think through what he wanted to say concerning his deep feelings about his father before talking to the children. Though every person has different feelings about people they love, this might be a typical way a father might tell his children about his thoughts on his own father: "You know that Grandpa is sick. It makes me feel a little scared and worried, too. Sometimes I feel angry that Grandpa has gotten sick, but most of all, I feel sad. When I was growing up, Grandpa was always the person who took care of things. Now that he can't, it makes me feel really bad. He was always so healthy and strong."

Though I knew Ethan was not eager to approach his children this way, I tried to explain that not only would he be helping his children understand his relationship to his father; he would be helping himself sort things out as well.

• *New Move 9: Let children visit a dying person, but spare them the graphic details of death.* Part of the preparation for someone's death are those last goodbye visits. Children, too, should be part of this process. Of course, there are limits to what they should see. A child shouldn't be allowed to visit when his loved one is in terrible pain, for example, or in the midst of suffering some of the indignities that particular treatment regimens can inflict on sick people. But children can see changes that illnesses cause. Two grandchildren I know told their grandfather who was undergoing chemotherapy, "Hey, Grandpa, your hair looks different and you're pretty skinny!" It broke some of the tension in the room, and their grandfather proceeded to launch into an age-appropriate explanation of why your hair falls out during chemotherapy. The kids were fascinated, and I suspect their grandfather felt better, too. Besides, they got to see the inside of the hospital; they watched doctors and nurses at work and learned that it wasn't such a scary place after all.

• *New Move 10: Explain the process of bereavement to children.* Continue to tell your children when you feel sad, even months after the death of a person you've loved. Explain that those lingering feelings are a normal part of saying goodbye to a person who has died. Alice, a woman I know, remembered as a child sitting one evening on the porch of a seashore house with a great-aunt whose sister had died the winter before. Alice's aunts had vacationed at the seashore every year. The aunt began to cry, remembering all the happy times they'd had, then turned to her young niece and said, "I really loved her and I just miss her a lot when I smell the salt air." That simple explanation, recalled by an Alice now grown, had told her a great deal about the bittersweet mixture of feelings people experience when someone close to them dies.

• *New Move 11: Continue to talk about a person who has died.* Teach children, as Alice's aunt did, that you can continue to talk about and have fond memories concerning a dead person, even if doing so may occasionally make you cry.

Keep photographs of the person around, reminisce and relate fond memories. You can say, "Remember how Grandma made those wonderful cookies at the holidays? Would you like to make some, too? Remember how she'd laugh when you got flour on your nose?" This will help your children accept that it's okay to talk about those who have died and may help them realize that the way dead people live on is in the memories of those they leave behind.

• *New Move 12: Be honest about tragic or sudden deaths.* All the same rules about being honest and forthright apply to telling children about deaths due to accident, violence, and sudden illness. Be aware that with unexpected deaths, children will have had no time to prepare, so their adjustment to the news may take longer and may be more painful. Younger children may find it especially difficult to acknowledge such a death. Of course, you can spare a child the graphic details of a violent death, just as you would spare them all the painful details of any death. If your child knows someone who died because of an accident, reassure her that even though accidents do occur, you as a family take every precaution to reduce the likelihood that one will happen to someone in your family. You might go over the family's safety rules and call your child's attention to the connection between drugs, alcohol, and accidents.

That something unexpected and out of control could happen worries children, because it suggests that adults, especially their parents, are not really capable of warding off all danger, and this leaves children frightfully vulnerable. Be careful not to add to these fears. The idea is to let them know that you are careful and will try your best to keep everyone safe and sound, but that even where accidents do occur most of them cause nothing more serious than a painful scratch or bruise.

AIDS is in the news a great deal, and whether or not you know an HIV-infected person, your children know something about the disease. Be honest with them. Children are receiving a great deal of public education these days, and many people are working to remove the stigma from that disease. You might say, "When people get AIDS, the fighter cells in their bodies stop working and they get a lot of sicknesses that healthy people's fighter cells destroy." Be honest about how people contract AIDS. They should know that it can be gotten through sexual contact, from injecting intravenous drugs with an infected needle, or, in fewer instances these days, from blood products. As uncomfortable as you may find a conversation about AIDS, your children need the facts.

8
Money and Employment

A man I know recently lost his job because of cutbacks at his company. I watched this normally cheerful, outgoing fellow turn inward as he struggled with all the emotions of such a moment. He felt hurt, bitter, even betrayed. "It's like a dream," he confided. "I'm just walking around in shock." When reality finally hit, it came in two painful doses. He not only wondered how he was going to pay all the bills; he also felt as though he had failed in his role of provider.

His children, a daughter eight and a son three, reacted true to form for their ages. The preschooler missed many of the details of the family crisis, but managed to remember one key phrase he'd heard his father muttering in exasperation: "No job, no money." He'd repeat it over and over again, not really understanding the full implication, knowing only that it was something that distressed his father. The eight-year-old, on the other hand, old enough to be genuinely worried about where the money would now come from to pay for things such as food and the rent, took the phrase much more to heart. With tears in her eyes, she rushed to reassure her father, "I don't care if I have to eat peanut butter and jelly for the rest of my life."

Your job, along with the money it provides, represents one of the cornerstones of family life. A job helps you define for your kids who you are and what you do out in the adult world. The money you earn has symbolic importance, playing a role in your relationship with your spouse, your relatives, and your neighbors. We invest tremendous emotional energy in the acquisition and outlay of money. And your kids know it, certainly by school age and often before. To them, money and job translate into where they live, the toys they have, the activities they can be a part of, the vacations the family takes, and even the food their parents buy for them. "When money isn't tight, we buy the fancy fresh-squeezed orange juice. But when we're sweating the bills, it's back to the frozen store brand," one father told me. "The kids pick up on that right away."

So if you have money problems, whether chronic blues over how you're going to pay the bills or worries about losing your job, don't be surprised when your children react to your anxiety. And this goes for common, everyday discontent with going to work, as well as how you react to moments of intense crisis. When they hear you ranting about your irrational boss or about how bored you are with the line of work you've chosen for yourself, your children may find themselves wondering if Peter Pan didn't have the right idea—maybe it's better not to grow up.

How you cope with your job-related problems and money troubles, and what you tell your children about facing such challenges can help them cope with similar challenges in their own lives. That is, if you do it right. You can teach your kids by example and explanation that such difficulties are not the end of the world but just a part of it.

This is not to say that financial problems won't sometimes cause painful changes that can be quite hard on a family. When Roberto lost his job his wife, Jennifer, went back to work full-time while Roberto cared for their eight- and six-year-olds. Just as the kids were adjusting to having Dad home in the afternoons, everything changed again. Roberto found shift work from three to eleven, though it didn't provide enough money to pay the bills and start working down the extra debt they had accumulated, and so Jennifer had to keep her job, too. Now the children learned they had to go to a day-care program after school. They barely saw Roberto during the week, and both parents were busy, distracted, and frazzled. The eight-year-old became unhappy, sullen, and argumentative; the six-year-old started getting headaches and crying. Both spent a lot of time fighting with each other and competing for their parents' scant time. These parents blamed themselves and were upset, depressed, and feeling the weight of all the pressure they were under. But even in a situation like this, parents can help children understand about tough times and pulling together as a family to get through.

What Children Learn from Their Parents about the Significance of Jobs and Money

The whole topic of money, including how you earn, save, and spend it, plays a large part in the values your children will end up with. They will notice if you are materialistic, if you watch every penny, if you use credit cards too freely or worry too much about the debt that results.

They'll also begin to realize that you may be sensitive about the status your job affords—or denies—you. One father I know, who is the maintenance supervisor for a large school district, bristled when one of his daughter's friends called him a school janitor. His daughter immediately sensed his anger. Kids can also learn from you whether you think fulfillment on the job is important. From your discussions about your job, they can learn many positive things, such as making commitments and sticking to them, following instructions, and achieving goals.

In addition, children quickly observe that money and jobs play a role in their parents' relationship and can be used as power ploys, such as when the higher or sole wage earner makes all the financial decisions. They'll also notice which of their parents is perceived to have the more important job. Money is also, of course, the source of much everyday bickering: "I can't believe you bought that! Why don't you go get a job if you must spend money so freely!"

Children also get strong messages from you about money's ability to define a person's worth to others. One mother told me that one of the hardest parts about losing her job was explaining to her eight-year-old son that she could no longer keep him up-to-date on the expensive electronic games he'd grown used to receiving regularly. "But, Mom," he wailed, "none of the other kids will like me if I don't have the good games." Probably in part because of her own vulnerability at that moment, she decided to forgo some necessities to buy him the games he wanted. But such a strategy can backfire. It may perpetuate her son's belief that his primary value to others depends on the material goods he can parade. Or that his mother agrees that he is the kind of kid who needs to buy friends.

By the way, children originally learn this lesson about life when they see you scrambling to keep up with the Joneses or hear you bemoaning your financial status and how it will affect your social standing. Though many of us have these feelings of competitiveness and self-worth connected to money and jobs, it is a mistake to voice them in front of our children. Such conversations may give children the impression that money and material things are the way people validate each other. And if you lose your job or have to live on less in order to make ends meet, your children will feel bereft and inferior because you've tied financial status so closely to self-worth.

Money is an emotionally charged topic in most families, even in the best of times. Parents often wonder how much to tell kids or let kids see concerning money or job issues, or at what age they can absorb it all. Here's a look at the different age groups and what each developmental stage brings with it in terms of children's knowledge and understanding of money and employment issues.

The Child's-Eye View

Unlike some of the other sensitive topics addressed in this book, money and its practical uses may be beyond the comprehension of most toddlers and many young preschoolers. But the effect of reduced or lost income on your lifestyle and your mood will be noticed by even the youngest children. Once your kids get to school age, they'll not only become more aware of money, but they'll also begin to notice your attitude toward your job and what it says about being an adult.

Toddlers

Though a toddler will have little understanding of money or your job problems, he will notice if his parents are upset or anxious over these issues. Food shopping, which he may adore, will lose its luster if you suddenly have to deny him the goodies he has been used to. Or he may notice that because you are tense over how to cover food expenses you snap at him more. If you come home at the end of the workday edgy and hostile, his natural feistiness at this age may drive you to distraction.

A toddler will not know what losing a job means, but he is likely to notice the few positive aspects to the situation if this happens in your family. Mom or Dad may be around the house more, so he's bound to feel happy about that. The parent who has lost the job is likely to be on edge, though, so it might not be as much fun as the toddler thought it would be. In addition to this, his regular routine, so important to a toddler, will almost definitely be disrupted. If Mom has been the primary caregiver and she suddenly gets a job, for example, having Dad as caregiver may initially be small comfort. He'll need time to get adjusted to the new routines.

Your toddler may show you that he is affected by your job or money stresses by regressing in toilet training, waking in the middle of the night, or becoming clingy and insecure.

Preschool-Age Children

A preschooler will have a somewhat more sophisticated understanding than a toddler of the relationship between your job and the money that buys her the things she needs and wants. You can show her your paycheck, or the cash you earn, and tell her that you received it for the work you did, but many preschoolers will continue to believe that the family gets the money it needs by writing a check or by going to the bank and withdrawing whatever is needed. One mother told me that when her husband's union went on an extended strike and she began to fret about money, her four-year-old said breezily, "Mom, why don't you just go to that machine in the wall at the bank and use that card to get money out?"

A preschooler may notice lifestyle changes that cause her some deprivation. If she has been used to your buying her a toy during trips to the mall, for example, she may feel some consternation when she realizes that she has to economize, too. Or if you blow up at her in frustration over her frequent requests for toys or outings you cannot afford, she may take your warnings at more than face value. She may start thinking there will never again be toys or treats.

If you hate your job, your preschooler will soon know it. Though she may not seem to relate it to her own life directly, she may pick up on your rage toward the control your boss has over your life and begin acting it out in her own play.

Young School-Age Children

By the time a child reaches school age, he's probably begun to be interested in the give-and-take of money. His interest in counting, coins, and an allowance all help increase his comprehension of what money means. He also better understands that a big reason his parents work is to earn the money that is then used to feed, clothe, and shelter him. At this age, he also begins to understand how you feel about your job and whether you feel satisfied with how you spend your work hours. After all, he's now involved in the day-to-day routine of school. He sees you going off to work each day, and he may closely observe your feelings about your responsibilities in relation to his own. If you're constantly ranting about how you hate your boss, he may begin to feel the same way about the authority figures in his life at school. The school-age child is also beginning to be aware of money arguments between his parents, and about which of the two has job status, and which makes the important financial decisions for the family.

If one of you loses your job, he may truly worry about whether the family will still be able to buy food and other necessities. One mother told me that when her husband lost his job, her son became immediately aware of how often they were eating canned soup and tuna fish, and worried about what would happen after the cans on the shelf were depleted. The eight-year-old who committed herself to peanut butter and jelly also displayed an understanding of the relationship between loss of work and necessities. School-age children are very aware of the homeless these days, and they may suddenly remember an explanation of homeless people that included the fact that many of them don't have jobs.

Because the school-age child is so much more aware of social aspects of money, she also may feel embarrassed if you have to economize. Her generic sneakers, her inability to have lessons her friends take for granted, and other lifestyle changes that will be obvious to her friends may really bother her. And if her usually absent parent is suddenly around more, she may wonder what her friends will think of that. One father told me that when he took a greater part in his son's school activities while he was between jobs, the boy felt embarrassed. They lived in a bedroom community, where most of the fathers traveled to the city to work. None of his friends' fathers ever took a turn at class parent, and he felt conspicuous when his father did.

Missteps Parents Make

When you lose your job, or you're feeling tense over work or money problems, you may become despondent or suffer a loss of self-esteem. Also, many parents get very emotional when they think about depriving their kids of the things they want and need, making it much more likely that you will say—or avoid saying—things about your money or your job that can really trouble your kids. Here are a few of the most common missteps parents make:

• *Hiding the loss of a job.* Some parents may feel that in order to not worry their children they'll just pretend to keep working. But think of how difficult the logistics will be. For instance, do you leave for the station as usual every morning? Do you pretend to arrive home on the five-thirty-eight? Trying to live out such a sham would be awful, and besides, your kids will probably figure it out within days, anyway. Intimations of it will be everywhere, from overheard conversations and increased tension between you and your spouse to watching you hesitate with knitted brow over an expensive imported fresh pineapple at the supermarket.

Setting aside for the moment all the extra stress you're putting on yourself by such shenanigans, treating children this way is not fair to them. They'll actually feel better if they see that even in tough times, you pull together as a family and work on the sacrifices together. Deprived of the true facts, they may feel you are hiding an even worse catastrophe from them. School-age children in particular will notice the sudden lack of funds if a vacation is canceled, for example, and wonder what major calamity has struck the family. Their imaginations can run wild waiting for the full force of the disaster to become evident.

• *Divulging too much about your financial worries after a job loss.*
While some parents are reluctant to talk about finances at
all, others cannot seem to help telling their children too
much. If you walk around the house after you lose your
job talking about what a tragedy has occurred and how
great a catastrophe has been visited upon the family, your
children will pick up on your cues and get very scared. The
same goes for rattling off a litany of things they'll no longer
be able to do or have. You may be talking about a short-
term period of deprivation until things sort themselves out
for you, but your children hear it as something they may
be facing for life.

By the way, don't feel compelled to tell your children
details about your assets or how much money you earn. It
will likely leak to others, and you'd rather not have such
precise information about your finances spread around. If
you're in a financial crunch and you don't want your children to worry, it's enough to tell them, "We have enough
money to pay for food and clothes and the house." It isn't
until young adulthood that your kids will be old enough to
handle information about your financial affairs without telling the world.

• *Blowing up at your kids when they ask for things.* When money
problems are worrying you, children's demands—or even
requests—for non-necessaries, such as toys and outings, can
make you see red. But young children have short memories
for distasteful admonitions, such as "We have to cut back
on family spending." What dominates their minds is the
barrage of messages in the television commercials for con-
sumer products, as well as the fact that the other kids in
their circle seem to be acquiring new things constantly.
Your children may feel upset and even angry at you for

depriving them of the things they used to take for granted, and in fact everyone else still does. It's hard not to start viewing your children as selfish and unfeeling, but they're just picking up on media cues telling them to buy, buy, buy. If you explode at them, they may begin to feel that your money problems are all their fault and feel guilty and anxious about their "greediness."

• *Bickering with your spouse about money problems in front of the children.* Blaming each other for all the family's financial problems is very troubling to your children. This is a topic on which they should see their parents working together. Instead, they witness divisiveness and disrespect. "Why don't you get a better job? . . . If you just earned more money, we wouldn't have these problems. . . . If you'd just get a job instead of sitting around all day, we'd be okay. . . . If you stopped spending so much money on clothes and spent some time managing our money, we'd be able to survive. . . . How could you have bought that? You spent way too much money!"

These kinds of demeaning statements can lead children to grow up believing that a parent was intentionally depriving them of things by not being hardworking, ambitious, or smart enough. In reality, the parent being accused may have been doing the best he or she could do. Or the children might come to believe that a non-wage-earning parent is selfish, thinking only of buying things rather than protecting the family finances. You and your spouse shouldn't throw such ugly charges at one another in any event, but it's particularly important not to do so in front of your children.

• *Ranting about your job problems in front of the kids.* If you spend all your time putting down your job, don't be surprised if your children grow up feeling that having a career is a pretty miserable experience. From there, it's a short hop to thinking that there is little happiness waiting for them when they grow up. I know two fathers who have drifted from job to job, never feeling satisfied with any. Both have said that they are doing exactly what their own fathers did. If you do hate your job and are helpless at this point to change your employment, try to focus on some other positive aspect about it, such as that it pays for your vacations or it enables you to live well. Or it may be that your job does not pay that well, but it allows you to do work that helps others. Children should glean from what you say that there is some meaning to what you do with your work hours beyond hating every minute you're there.

New Moves

Instead of dreading the task of telling your children about financial problems, see it as an opportunity. Some parents may feel embarrassed about losing their jobs and worry that their kids will think of them as failures. But if explained carefully, a job loss or other financial problem may provide an opportunity to show your children that you, too, can run into problems. Most kids think their parents do everything perfectly, especially tasks that still challenge or frustrate children. After all, you can tie your shoes, zip up jackets in a second, add and subtract and read. It wouldn't be a bad thing for them to see that not everything in your life works out with effortless ease. What's more important, they'll see that you pick yourself up and go on. That's not a bad model to provide your kids as they face their own challenges in school and at play.

Here's how to explain hard financial facts without fanning their fears.

• *New Move 1: Be open about a job loss.* Your kids should see that you can talk about it matter-of-factly. If you do feel panicky when you first find out, you might want to think through your plans before you tell your children what has happened. They will feel less frightened if you come to them with a handle on what you intend to do about your misfortune. Give them a simple explanation as to why you lost your job, one that a preschooler or school-age child can understand. You might say, "I lost my job because my company closed," or, "There were more people at my company than they wanted or could pay for, so some of us had to go." If you have lost your job due to poor performance or prickly relations with a boss, you might say, "I wasn't ready for the job I had. I thought I was, but I found out otherwise. I really will be better off doing something I'm better at." Or: "I really didn't get along with the person I worked for. He wanted to work with someone else, and I will find someone I can work better with."

• *New Move 2: Reassure your children that you will all survive a job loss.* Though you may be feeling nervous, crushed, or depressed, you should try to keep an upbeat, optimistic attitude when explaining things to your children. You might tell them, "Life has different obstacles and setbacks. This hasn't been the first and it won't be the last. But we can get through it." Tell your children, especially school-age children who understand what your paycheck provided, how you will continue to pay for your basic needs, such as food and housing. Maybe your company gave you severance pay, or your union has a strike fund you can mention. Or explain that there are some savings to dip into. Sometimes children will ask if there's anything they can do to help, offering you their small savings. If it's just a few pennies from a preschooler, I'd just take them and say thanks. It's a sweet gesture and you wouldn't want him to feel his offering was rejected. But tell your school-age child to keep her saved allowance money. You might say, "Things aren't that bad yet, but I appreciate your willingness to pitch in. That's just the sort of spirit our family needs." This will reassure an older child who may be worrying about the extent of the trouble you're in financially.

• *New Move 3: When a job loss occurs, explain your game plan for the future, along with the changes your children can expect.* A game plan is comforting to children. They see that you aren't just being buffeted around by forces beyond your control. Explain how you are going about finding a new job, providing some concrete detail about résumés, interviews, and the classified section of the newspaper. Let them know right away about big lifestyle changes. If a parent who was at home will be going to work full-time, explain who will be taking care of them. Many kids are delighted to find out that their previously working parent will be doing some child-care duties. Others may need time to adjust to the change, especially if the parent who will be spending more time with them is tense and irritable because he's lost his job.

Prepare children for the lifestyle changes that economizing will bring. If it means fewer toys or name-brand items they like, and no vacation, they'll be less shocked if they're prepared and forewarned. Be sure to point out that the changes won't last forever. And come up with some economical substitutes, such as going to the beach or on trips to the park or a museum. If it looks as though your long-term financial future is not rosy, you may be thinking about moving to save money. Unless you see this as imminent, I wouldn't mention it to your kids at the outset. Moving is a big deal for children and can be very traumatic, especially if the move will take them to a new neighborhood and new schools. But if you believe you will have to move, prepare your kids for that possibility. Though they will have concerns and worries, the preparation will help them see it as part of the family's plan for staying financially solvent.

• *New Move 4: Explain to your children why you feel edgy and tense when you've lost your job.* When you lose your job, you not only worry about money but may also go through a complex array of emotions leading to doubt about yourself and your abilities. Though you want to remain upbeat about the future, there's nothing wrong with explaining to your children some of the reasons for your grouchiness. You might tell them that losing a job is often more than just losing the money it provides. Even if you don't believe that your job defined you, tell them you were achieving things, producing things, or helping people, and that your work made you feel productive. There's nothing wrong with feeling some sadness or bitterness over a job loss, and you can certainly tell your children that. Such an explanation can be tailored even to a preschooler's level. Use this opportunity to tell them that because of all this you may find it hard to be cheerful at times. Don't be afraid to ask your kids to cut you a little more slack through this period.

If work plays a major role in your definition of yourself, and you're feeling a loss of self-esteem, you might tell your children, "I studied a long time, practicing and learning skills that I needed for my work. People told me I did a good job and they paid me well for it. I feel bad when I'm not using my skills, and I feel better when I am working." You might also tell your kids that you miss the sociability that work provides. Ask them how they'd feel if they suddenly didn't see their friends or go to school. Tell them you get to play different grown-up roles at work, much as they get to act differently at school than they do at home. Now you miss all that, and so you feel grumpy sometimes. Finally, let your kids know that searching for a new job can be hard. You might say, "You know how hard it is on the first day of school, when you're just meeting your teacher, or you're in a different class and have to meet strange new kids. That's what it's like in a job interview. No one knows you and you have to tell strangers about yourself."

• *New Move 5: Give your children updates if your job search or financial difficulties go on for a long time.* Kids should be privy to some of the details of your ongoing job search. They don't need all the blow-by-blow details of every interview, and they shouldn't be waiting with baited breath by the door after each one, but you can tell the kids that you are still going on interviews, working diligently to find a job, and that your spirits are still high.

Though no one likes to see his children worry, it's okay for kids to see that life can sometimes be a struggle. They will learn that part of life is overcoming adversity and that it won't always be easy for them, either. By continuing to search for a job, you're showing them that you have the resources to overcome the obstacles. When you explain the different tactics and strategies you're trying in order to locate a job, they'll see how things are done in the real world. Keeping the discussion out in the open, rather than confining yourself to whispered talks with your spouse or with older children only, will help younger kids see that they can bring the topic up if their fantasies start to bother them too much. And you can tell them that you feel bad sometimes, too. But continue to explain to your older children how you are getting by financially, so they won't worry.

• *New Move 6: Explain the concept of family sacrifice to children.* When you're in a financial crunch and you have to economize, let your children know that you're grateful for their patience and sacrifices. Be firm when they ask for things, but try to explain gently how all of you have to sacrifice. Kids sometimes take things personally, and they may begin to think you're depriving them on purpose because they were bad and should be punished for bringing on the family troubles. At other times, they will believe that you have everything and they have nothing. Sympathize with their frustration and point out that there are some things that you'd like to buy, too, but simply cannot afford right now. One mother I know occasionally says things like "See those shoes? I'd really like to buy them, but I can't right now because we're really trying to save our money." Her son finds it comforting to know that he isn't the only one feeling disappointed and deprived.

• *New Move 7: Teach children that parents can disagree over money without acrimony.* It's okay to disagree over money in front of children. It just depends on how you do it. A couple I know who are feeling financially pinched told me that they regularly have a "new couch" discussion in front of their children. One spouse will advocate getting the much needed couch, and the other will gently bring up the fact that they really cannot afford it right now.

By allowing their children to see family financial decisions debated and resolved, this couple is teaching their children that you can't have everything you want whenever you want it. If you do have such debates in front of your children, be sure that they see how you resolve them. If the couple decide to save a hundred dollars a month toward the couch and buy it next year, their children will get a good lesson in deferred spending. Most important, they'll get to see that their parents are pulling together and acting as a team, and that they can reach a compromise even when they start off on an issue with very different ideas.

• *New Move 8: Don't deprive yourself of all enjoyment if you have financial problems.* Many parents who are facing financial difficulties feel that all the joy in life must suddenly come to a halt. Grim duty takes over, and they act as if good times are behind them, back in another life. Kids feel this acutely. Instead, point out to your children that you can still plan inexpensive day trips or have nice dinners at home that don't cost a fortune. It would not be a bad idea to point out to them that many people on this earth manage to have good and happy family lives on less money than your family has available to it during this emergency. They should see that with more or less money, life goes on, and that you don't feel that all is lost just because you don't have as much money to spend as you'd like to have.

9
Substance Use and Abuse

Last night you lugged home a bulging briefcase containing at least three hours of work you hoped to get to as soon as your four- and six-year-olds were in bed. But half an hour after you tucked them in, your son began vomiting, and he continued to do so, on and off, until the wee hours. Now morning is here and not only is your work unfinished, you are exhausted to boot. Fighting with your daughter to get her off to school on time and arranging with your reluctant mother to babysit your ailing son don't improve your disposition.

Though every night of parenthood isn't as bad as this one, it's no secret that today's parents face countless everyday stresses that contribute to the ongoing problem of drug, alcohol, and tobacco abuse in our society. Jobs and households need attention, but so do the kids. Your parents are aging and may need your help, too. Money anxieties and relationship problems enter into many marriages, and then there are all the challenges of single parenting with which today's parents have to cope.

For many people, the solution is an age-old one: have a drink, smoke a joint or a cigarette, or take a pill. Life is so full of worries that seem to defy resolution that substance use can have an appeal as a not-so-bad short-term answer. It's a long way from use to abuse, we know, from the occasional before-dinner cocktail to daily heavy drinking or reliance on other drugs, and we are sure we know just how far we can safely go and still not find ourselves on that slippery slope we know exists at the far end of the spectrum.

Wherever you are on the spectrum, however, you should be considering the effect that such practices have on your young children. Aside from how well you can handle your own use of cigarettes, alcohol, and drugs, there remains a critical question for all parents who rely on stress-relieving chemicals: What are you teaching your children about coping with stress? It is not enough to say that feelings such as anger, sadness, and anxiety often lead people to turn to alcohol or drugs, or to light up a cigarette. What second-level message does this explanation send your children about the lifestyle you have chosen for yourselves?

A woman I know who is currently under a great deal of stress told me that her six-year-old daughter recently asked, "Mommy, why have you started drinking wine with dinner?" This school-age child may not have understood all the implications of alcohol use, but she clearly noticed that her mom had developed a new habit. It's interesting to consider whether she would have been as aware of the change if her mother had suddenly started drinking milk with dinner. Kids understand more than we imagine about why we do what we do, and this particular child happened to know that her mother had been anxious and tense lately.

Many of today's parents worry about how to talk to kids about cigarettes, drugs, and alcohol. Many feel confused and conflicted, remembering their own youthful drug use and how their own parents handled—or mishandled—the subject. They worry that they, too, will wind up sounding like a hypocrite: "Do as I say, not as I do." And there is some real justification for that fear, because kids do model their parents' behavior, for good or for bad. Telling them not to smoke, for example, while you continue to puff away is not going to achieve much.

Not only is there the possibility that your kids will see you as a hypocrite, but you may be in for some other criticism as well. "We call our kids the smoking police," comments one father dryly. Television is jammed with anti-drug references, and kids are becoming involved in drug-education and smoking-prevention programs at school at very young ages. Once they've learned about the risks of passive smoke inhalation, they may accuse you of willfully harming their health. Yet despite all these efforts at prevention, reports of drug and alcohol abuse and cigarette smoking among teenagers are so frightening that parents of young children continue to fret that their own children will soon be adding to the ugly statistics. Parents are wondering how they can prepare their children for the temptations they'll soon be exposed to, in a way that will continue to protect them when they reach the most vulnerable adolescent years. One parent told me that at a recent school-board meeting in her small town, parents of grade-schoolers crowded the room because they had heard that there was an alcohol problem at the high school. These parents wanted to know what the board planned to do concerning prevention programs at the grade-school level to try to head off problems in the future.

You may be worrying about the effect on your children of your own use of drugs, alcohol, or cigarettes. Or you may be wondering how to talk to your children about substance abuse in general. But before we begin to explore ways to talk and act, let's look at what children learn from their parents' use of drugs and alcohol.

A Child's View of Your Need for Mood-Altering Substances

A discussion of what to do in front of the kids, and say to them, concerning substance use and abuse may, more than most of the other subjects in this book, require that you examine some of your most closely held attitudes about dealing with life's stresses. One of the main reasons people reach for various substances is to dull or mask feelings too difficult to confront. They do so out of a mistaken notion that life's challenges should provide little stress and no pain. We feel resentful and assume that something is wrong with our lives if, on any sort of a regular basis, problems arise that cause us distress. Some people actually feel jinxed, or resent others whose lives seem to go more smoothly.

The degree to which you use mood-altering substances, including nicotine, as a way of coping puts you in one of several camps, ranging from those who won't even touch caffeine, to people who are garden-variety indulgers, to alcoholics and drug abusers who clearly have problems that daily threaten to destroy the family. If you believe that you rely on these substances more than you'd like to, and worry about the effect on your children as well as yourself, you may have to give some thought to restructuring your life, so that you can begin facing feelings you formerly covered up with cigarettes, drugs, or alcohol.

If you are successful in your efforts, you'll be teaching your children a priceless lesson—that life is not conflict-free, that conflict can be within one person as well as between people, and that either way it can be dealt with. If your example reinforces what you say to them, you'll be teaching them that there are ways to tolerate stress besides trying to mask it by abusing various substances. Your kids will learn that uncomfortable feelings aren't necessarily bad, certainly not so bad that they have to be suppressed at all costs.

Many parents, concerned that their children will get upset if they see Mom and Dad fretting or worrying over life's frustrations and setbacks, may resort to smoking, taking drugs, or having a few drinks to calm themselves down. But when you confront your problems and fashion solutions to them, rather than trying always to escape or mask them, you'll show your children how people can use stress as a motivation to change things in ways that reduce or eliminate the causes of the stress. Many psychologists believe that if you are never frustrated, you'll never grow emotionally. Overcoming obstacles and learning new approaches to dealing with your problems may not always be easy or pain-free, but kids should know that life isn't solely about feeling good. Moreover, the "good feeling" you get from cigarettes, drugs, and alcohol is, in fact, more a dulling of the senses or a temporary checkout from reality—either result a far cry from that true sense of happiness you experience when you have your life organized so that it is not always threatening to blow up in your face.

But be prepared for the future. Even if you are successful in conveying to your children that it's better to confront difficulties than to sweep them under the carpet, they may still experiment with cigarettes, drugs, or alcohol when they reach adolescence. This is because, aside from their ability to end a "down" feeling, even though only temporarily, these drugs are seductive in that they enable teens to experience pleasant sensations of calm, elation, or power. These are sought-after feelings during adolescence, whether or not the adolescent is trying to escape reality.

Even the most emotionally healthy kid may be tempted to try drugs at some point during adolescence. If you've done your best to help your kids learn to deal with their problems, the period of experimentation will probably be no more than a phase. Stay calm, talk to your kids, and try to remember that it's a predictable part of adolescence.

There will be an additional benefit for those parents who are prepared to give up their own bad habits to help their children avoid substance abuse in the future: an improvement in the well-being of everyone in your household. Smokers who quit lessen the risk of having a family member develop lung cancer or emphysema, as well as reduce the many well-known risks to the smoker himself. Drug and alcohol users can reduce their risk of becoming involved in accidents and of developing many other medical conditions.

In short, you have nothing to lose and everything to gain by beginning to examine your relationship with various substances. Before talking about the common missteps and new moves parents can make in direct dealings with their children, here's a look at how substance use and abuse is interpreted by children.

The Child's-Eye View

Let's look at how toddlers, preschoolers, and young school-age children comprehend and interpret what they see and hear regarding parental substance use in general, and their likely reactions if there is a problem in your family.

Toddlers

Toddlers have very little awareness of a parent's substance-abuse habits, but they will certainly recognize when Mom is behaving oddly. The child may not know the difference between a seltzer and a gin-and-tonic or the significance of a third drink, but if a parent has reached the point where drinking or drugs are causing him or her to be inattentive to an active toddler, the child will feel emotionally neglected. Her parent still feeds and bathes her, but is so preoccupied that she or he doesn't give the emotional support a toddler needs to feel secure as she grows. Older toddlers may show signs of regression, such as tantrums or clinginess. If drug or alcohol use causes a parent to snap into great rages of anger, a toddler can become apprehensive and scared of her parent. There is, of course, the additional reality that the child may come to some physical harm as a consequence of the lack of parental supervision.

Preschool-Age Children

A preschooler will begin to understand the connection between taking medicine and feeling better. When she has a cold, you give her cough syrup; a headache warrants a pain reliever. Even food, though it shouldn't be presented this way, is often used as a way of comforting a preschooler with a problem. She may begin to ask for that magic pill, potion, or food to relieve her pain or discomfort, physical or emotional. Though she is not yet aware that you and your spouse have magic substances of your own, a preschooler will begin to notice, to a much greater degree than a toddler, if you are preoccupied or inattentive. Naturally, we're all this way sometimes, but if the effects of a drinking or drug habit cause you to become numbed to your own feelings about other problems and responsibilities, your preschooler will notice this quickly. If you're out of sync with your child's feelings and needs, he's likely to become insecure, clingy, and whiny, or begin acting up in nursery school, hurting a younger sibling, or picking fights with an older sibling.

A recovering alcoholic I know told me a story that occurred while she was still drinking. She was sitting at the table one morning, nursing a hangover, when her four-year-old came down for breakfast. She gave him a distracted hug and poured him some cereal. Then she sat back down and stared at her toast and juice. The little boy ate a few bites, then said worriedly, "Mom, aren't you going to have breakfast with me?" Though this mother was sitting right next to her son, drinking her juice and occasionally tossing out a few "uh-huhs" to his running commentary, he reacted as if she weren't really sitting there with him.

If drug or alcohol use affects your moods, it's at this age that a child may begin to worry that your angry outbursts are her fault. You're hung over, but your child doesn't know how you got that way. He wonders what he did to cause your irritability. Or he begins to be mystified over your unpredictability. One day when he spills the milk, you just clean it up together. The next day, you rage at him.

Of course, we all have mood swings that will change the way we behave toward everyone, our children included. But the moods of people who abuse drugs or alcohol are always swinging, and wildly, from extreme to extreme. Inappropriate emotional reactions such as laughing hysterically at things that are not especially funny also give away that things are not right with you. As yet, however, preschoolers are too young to understand why their parents are behaving inconsistently.

Young School-Age Children

By this point in their young lives, children have begun to notice a great deal about their parents' behaviors and habits. They begin to ask what's in the glass. They may ask you point-blank why you drink, especially if drinking is an established ritual in your house. Or if they stumble across drug paraphernalia, they may remember having seen it on TV or as part of a drug-education program. It's at this age that kids begin to look for how their parents deal with pain and sadness, because they are beginning to feel some stress of their own at school.

Your school-age child may begin to pressure you to give up some of your bad habits, such as smoking, because of what she's learning at school. I'm not sure that's an altogether bad thing, since researchers who study the most effective ways to help people quit smoking say that the more uncomfortable the habit becomes, the more likely people are to quit. So you may want to honor your school-age child's request that you not smoke in the house.

Few young school-age children will be able to make the connection between your consumption of alcohol and your subsequent mood. When you think about it, many adults are hard pressed to see the connection between things they consume and subsequent physical reactions. People who are allergic to certain foods, for example, may not realize immediately that there's a connection. So it would be expecting a lot of a grade-schooler to understand the cause-and-effect relationship between a parent's consumption of alcohol and the way the parent behaves toward the child in the hours afterward.

How Drug Abuse and Alcoholism Affect Children

Much has been written about the devastating effect an alcohol- or drug-abusing parent can have on his or her children. One of the main problems is that parents, both the abuser and the spouse, may try to hide from their children the extent of the abuse. But even if you are able to hide the bottles or the drug paraphernalia, school-age children will still pick up the clues that something is very wrong. A woman I know whose mother was an alcoholic remembered that her mother slept late, even on school days, and that she couldn't seem to rouse her from her sleep. She didn't know why at first, but she did know something was wrong, that most kids had a parent to help them get breakfast and prepare for school. More often than not, she had to fix her own lunch as well as her breakfast, and had to remember to brush her teeth and comb her hair.

Feeling Different

At just the age when they want to conform and be like other kids, school-age kids with a substance-abusing parent begin to get a sense that their lives are different from those of other kids. Daddy falls asleep over dinner, or Mommy slurs her words a lot and she's forgetful. Paul remembers his drunk father knocking over the Christmas tree when Paul was a young school-ager. Paul doubted his own sense of reality at the time, because the family was collectively denying the facts. Is there something wrong, or isn't there? he recalls asking himself.

Feeling Unnoticed

The deception required to maintain such a household often turns school-age children into frequent liars. For one thing, their parents are too preoccupied to notice the development, and honesty doesn't seem to have much value anyway. A man I know whose father was an alcoholic remembers skipping his Sunday school class for weeks and weeks without his parents ever noticing. Each Sunday, the boy would make up a story about what he'd learned that day. He recalls that, eventually, lying immediately came to mind in any situation where the truth was uncomfortable. He got very good at small and large deceptions, which he'd sometimes try just to see if he could get away with them. Most of the time, he did.

Feeling Uncared For

Children whose parents are caught up in a cycle of alcohol or drug dependency don't have a strong sense that anyone is caring for them. In fact, they feel an enormous responsibility for a lot of things that shouldn't be theirs to worry about. They become protectors of a drug- or alcohol-abusing parent, fending off phone calls, letting their parent sleep, becoming overly self-reliant at too young an age. They take on duties that properly belong to their parents. The woman who as a young child had to fix her own lunch remembers assuming that responsibility for her younger siblings as they started school.

Feeling Guilty

School-age children also blame themselves for their parents' drug or alcohol problems. They're constantly trying to figure out what they did to provoke a drunken rage or a binge. Ironically, pressures that parents try so desperately to mask

with alcohol or drugs grow worse from neglect, and the
child begins to feel like just one more burden added to the
ever-increasing pressure. As well as guilt, he's learning
something else: his parent uses drugs or alcohol to deal
with pressure. The child may do the same himself when he
gets older.

Feeling Scared and Confused

Finally, life becomes unbearably unpredictable. Dad may
be too stoned or drunk to drive his son and his friends to
the skating rink, but the child won't know for sure until it's
time to leave. Mom may not be okay to take him to his
Scouts meeting. He doesn't know if today will be a good
day or a bad one.

Far-Reaching Effects

The future for children who grow up in such households
can be bleak. A lifetime of watching adults running away
from normal feelings can render children incapable of expressing their own feelings. No one has ever taught them
that uncomfortable feelings are really okay, or that they
can deal with them in healthy ways. They themselves may
become substance abusers as a result. In later years, many
have trouble with adult relationships, because their own
sense of security was so compromised in their primary relationships with their parents. The ones who took their
prematurely fostered responsibility seriously may grow into
obsessively responsible adults, overly controlling, unable
ever to let go for a second. Others may take their parents'
cues and renege on their responsibilities altogether. In
either case, such people tend to judge themselves harshly
on all fronts, because they're still convinced that it was something they did that caused all the problems at home. They

tend to blame themselves even in situations where someone else is clearly at fault.

If you or your spouse is abusing alcohol or drugs, I urge you to get help, for your own sake and for the sake of your children. Alcohol and drug recovery and support groups have helped millions of people begin the road to health. Spouses of substance abusers should also seek help through groups that support the families of addicted people. Later in this chapter, I'll suggest some New Moves that recovering alcohol and drug abusers can make to begin reestablishing ties with their children.

Missteps Parents Make

Many, many people rely, to one degree or another, on various substances to relieve the stress of everyday living. Confronting and dealing with the stresses in your life that activate your own drinking or drug use may require that you pay a price in time, effort, and sometimes emotional pain. But whether you make these efforts or not, you should begin thinking about the messages that your behavior toward drugs and alcohol sends to your kids. Unwittingly, you may be conveying attitudes that can affect their later use of cigarettes, drugs, and alcohol. Here are a few common missteps.

• *Reaching in front of the children for a drink, cigarette, pills, or other substances when you're upset or anxious.* Your children shouldn't learn that you have to smoke a cigarette or swig a drink in order to deal with—or avoid—stress. A woman I know vividly remembers her father bursting in the door each day muttering, "After the day I had at the office, I need a drink." Nor should you joke about your need for these things to help you manage stress. And be careful about taking a drink for "courage" or "to relax" before a party, especially if your children are within earshot. All these actions suggest to your children that you don't have the wherewithal to confront uncomfortable feelings head on. And this suggests that they, your children, may not have those resources, either.

• *Overmedicating your children to relieve their stresses.* Though certainly there are times when children need pain relievers or cough syrup, don't rush to treat every little ache and pain with a magic potion. Parents who are quick to treat their own symptoms of physical and emotional pain may do the same to their children. A woman I know recalled that in her family, which included two alcoholic parents, huge amounts of over-the-counter medicines were taken for every small complaint. Food was also used as a comfort and pain reliever. Anything, she said, to keep her from feeling bad was preferable to talking through or confronting a problem.

• *Making alcohol an overwhelming presence on all occasions, including the end of every day and the beginning of every weekend.* Alcohol, because it is legal and so widely accepted almost everywhere, presents special problems concerning the message it sends to children. The more ritualized and ingrained your drinking is, the harder it is for children to imagine that life is ever complete without it. If your kids see that your weekend doesn't begin until you stop at the liquor store, they receive a very definite message. One man I know recalled that his parents' trips to the liquor store were such a big part of his life that as a first-grader he named the man in the liquor store as a community helper, right up there with the mail carriers and the firefighters.

A father I know, whose own parents had drinking problems, says he grew up believing that most occasions, including holidays and everyday dinners, should revolve
around the drinks served. It seemed to him that people
didn't start having a good time until they'd had a few drinks.
When he reached the age when liquor became accessible
for him, he quickly integrated it into all of his happy times,
too. This meant that as a teenager he often drove while
drunk and took other risks he shudders at today. A non-
drinker now, he finds that when he enters his parents' house
he still automatically thinks about what drink he'll ask for.

• *Giving children sips of alcoholic drinks.* Some parents still
believe that if you keep children away from alcohol, the
taboo will make them want it more. But it just isn't so.
Children should be told that alcohol, in moderation, is for
adults only. A household where it's okay for the kids to
imbibe, even as a joke, gives tacit acceptance to alcohol
consumption in underage children.

• *Using illegal drugs in front of the children, or leaving drug
paraphernalia around.* You may think that the laws against
substances such as marijuana are unfair and hypocritical,
given our government's massive acceptance of alcohol, but
at least in front of the children you should respect the law.
Whether or not you think some of our laws concerning
drugs are hypocritical, a presumption that a democratically
enacted law should be respected underlies democracy, and
parents have an obligation to teach this to their children.
That doesn't mean you can't talk to them about working to
change laws you don't agree with, or to point out that some
laws are so immoral that they cry out for civil disobedience.
But your children should understand that simply breaking
the law on the sly can never be classified as civil disobedi-

ence, for it does nothing to bring about the repeal of the immoral law. And, of course, getting around drug laws is still another problem, for no matter how some people defend their right to use drugs, the fact is that all purchases of illegal drugs support criminal activities that are regularly carried out as part of the distribution system. Remember that whatever sense of right and wrong you convey to your kids will become the basis for how they live their own lives. You certainly don't want to receive a middle-of-the-night call from a police station because your teenager decided in all his wisdom that one law or another was not worthy of his support.

• *Avoiding the truth about a spouse's drinking or drug problem, when your children know something is wrong.* Though it is a difficult and painful task, spouses of substance abusers should talk to their children, especially when they reach school age, about the problem the other parent has with alcohol or drugs. To this day, says one angry woman I know, her family talks about her mother's alcoholism as a diabetes condition.

To avoid so important a reality in their lives teaches kids that life at home is simply a façade. As children, and later as adults, they will be angry that you had so little respect for them that you refused to recognize their ability to understand reality. They may have a difficult time forgiving you for not acknowledging the problem and the price they as children were forced to pay because of it. Your intention may be to protect them from pain, but it feels to them that you're covering up and, in doing so, depriving them of the right to have their own pain and suffering witnessed and validated.

• *Avoiding kids' questions about why you drink or smoke.* Kids are quick studies. They do not fail to notice your dependency (or your spouse's) on various substances. If when they ask you why you need to drink or smoke you snap angrily, "That's none of your business," you'll convey the feeling that this is a touchy subject, something about which you're overly sensitive. Even if you simply say, "Don't worry about it, it's my problem," you're still leaving your kids to figure it out on their own. They may begin to feel that they're outside your inner circle, that you don't feel close enough to them to confide in them. You've shut them out of a segment of your life that is clearly important to you.

• *Continuing to smoke while admonishing your children to avoid the habit.* This just will not work. Not only will your children notice that you smoke to relieve stress and anxiety, but they will have an entire childhood filled with watching you smoke. Have you ever noticed your child using a pencil or even candy cigarettes in imitation of your smoking? It's the old story: your example is much more powerful than your words.

New Moves

Though many substance abusers may fret that their behavior has already done their children irreversible harm, they should know that at any point in the growing-up process they can help their kids if they change their behavior. Here are the new moves to make.

• *New Move 1: Teach your children emotional honesty.* When you're upset and stressed out, tell your children why. Then share with them the ways in which you work out a solution. If you're angry with someone, explain that you're going to talk to that person. If you hate your job, show them what you're doing to find a new one. If you're worried about money, explain how you're revising the family budget. Sometimes the lesson will be that all problems don't have easy solutions, or that solutions to difficult problems often take time, but they'll see you facing disappointment or anger or other uncomfortable feelings, and they'll learn to do it, too.

• *New Move 2: Show kids how you cope positively with the effects of stress.* If you're really angry, you can tell your kids you're going for a walk to sort out your feelings. Or explain that your evening run helps you relax and shed the worries of your workday. You can explain that in order to work on a particularly difficult problem you're going to see a therapist (be sure to explain that a therapist is someone who helps you to work out your problems). Explain how valuable friends can be when you have troubles. Show your kids how you write about your feelings in a journal or paint pictures to relax. When your kids come to you with a problem, use the opportunity to introduce them to effective coping techniques. Above all, reassure your kids that problems are surmountable, by saying things such as: "Look, I feel bad, but I will get through it."

• *New Move 3: Show by your example that drinking and drug use are not essential for happy times.* There's certainly nothing wrong with offering drinks to friends on occasion, or with having a drink yourself. But let your kids see that you offer nonalcoholic drinks, such as seltzer and juice, too. So many people in our society have sworn off drinking, it shouldn't be hard to show your kids some examples of people who come to parties and dinners and manage to have a great time without getting high. Your kids should see that even if you drink, you accept that other people may not. Along these lines, don't be aggressive in encouraging repeat drinks, unless you continue to offer nonalcohol alternatives as well, for you should avoid communicating to your children that the role of the host is to make sure that every guest gets sufficiently boozed up. Rethink the idea of putting out a full bar when people come to visit. When you control the refills, you set a subtle limit on how much people drink and the bar ceases to be the focal point of the party.

• *New Move 4: If you smoke, show your kids that you are making some effort to curb your habit.* Of course, the best thing would be for you to quit completely, but even if you cannot do that right away, show them that you are imposing limits on yourself. Excuse yourself and do your smoking outside. Promise that you will never smoke in the car. Order some of the smoking-cessation kits that are offered by various health organizations. Or join a program at work. Showing your child that you are struggling to quit will help resolve some of the contradiction in your continued smoking in the face of admonitions to the children not to take up the habit.

• *New Move 5: Explain to kids how the media often incorrectly portray alcohol consumption as a route to happy times and as a stress reliever.* Though media images of drug taking as an acceptable practice are fading fast, there are still a lot of people reaching for alcohol. One mother I know, who is careful about what and how she drinks in front of her seven-year-old daughter, was surprised to hear the little girl commenting on a scene from *My Fair Lady*, a video she'd grown fond of watching. "Henry Higgins needs that drink to give him courage to take Eliza to the ball," she said knowingly. A few days later, this same little girl, who admittedly watches a lot of old movies, was looking at *It's a Wonderful Life*. When the movie showed Jimmy Stewart going to a bar, she said, "He's sad, and he doesn't know what to do, so he's having a drink." You should point out to children that movie and television stories, especially those from the old days, sometimes show characters using alcohol when they're upset because in those days many people didn't yet understand that alcohol doesn't cure depression. But explain that we now know more about alcohol, that in real life it doesn't solve problems. You can add that we know that, if anything, turning to alcohol just makes it harder to think up a solution. You should talk to them about those TV commercials for beer and wine that convey the idea that all happy events are accompanied by drinking. Tell them that advertisers would like people to believe this so that they'll buy the company's beer or wine. But explain that many people have a good time without any alcohol.

• *New Move 6: Be honest about a parent who has a drinking or drug problem. Explain but don't excuse.* Kids desperately need to know the truth about a parent's substance-abuse problems, so that they don't start mistrusting their sense of reality. Many spouses of abusers wonder what exactly to say, whether it's okay to ask your children to forgive or understand that the other parent is sick.

This topic comes up especially in families where the substance abuser becomes physically or verbally abusive, hitting or shouting at the children. Spouses need to do two things if this occurs. You need to explain to your children that the reason for such abusive behavior is the drug or alcohol problem of the parent. Then you should add that such behavior is unacceptable. To ask a child to excuse such behavior is to condone it. Whenever a parent goes into a drunken rage, the other parent must remove the children from the situation by leaving the room or, if necessary, the house. Children must be convinced that someone is available to protect them from verbal and physical harm. Reassure them that you will continue to take care of them and try to get the other parent to obtain some help.

• *New Move 7: Don't try to shield the kids from the connection between drunken or high behavior and substance abuse.* In fact, children should understand all the destructive consequences of substance abuse. To counter ongoing media images that often show alcohol drinking as a harmless and even glamorous pastime, be sure to point out what can happen when you lose control of your life to one of the addictive substances. You might also point out the effects of smoking on people's skin and teeth, since kids are likely to understand such obvious and concrete changes. If a relative who smoked died of lung cancer or emphysema, point out the relationship of the disease to smoking. A man I know, whose father had been a heavy smoker for decades and had recently died of lung cancer, told his children that smoking caused the disease. As a result, the children, who watched their grandfather deteriorate, now tell people, "Granddad died from smoking." It may seem heartless to have the children see their grandfather as the causal agent of his own destruction, but the lesson the children are learning may save their own lives one day.

• *New Move 8: Use whatever help is available to explain the effects of cigarettes, drugs, and alcohol to school-age kids.* You might try contacting your school to see if there is a manual available for parents on how to provide age-appropriate

explanations of drugs and their effects. Here's the kind of
guidance you should give your children, especially after
they reach grade-school age and begin to spend some time
on their own:

1. Explain what different drugs, such as marijuana, co-
   caine, and crack look like (some manuals for parents
   have pictures that you can show your kids).
2. Emphasize that although alcohol is legal for adults it
   is an illegal drug for children.
3. Tell your children about the many chemical changes
   these drugs cause in your body and how each harms
   the human body. Make sure you include information
   about the emotional effects of drugs. You might explain that many drugs make you feel good at first, but
   then worse when the drug wears off. You could add
   that some drugs make you feel so powerful that you
   might attempt dangerous or reckless things while under their influence.
4. Explain that even good medicines, taken in too large
   doses, can be dangerous drugs, too. Many kids think
   that if a little bit of medicine is good, then a lot must
   be better.

• *New Move 9: Assure kids that they can always talk to you about
scary or bad things that happen to them.* If you remain a receptive audience for all of your children's questions and
problems you will encourage them to keep the lines of
communication open through adolescence. A woman I
know who has always been honest and up-front with her
son about difficult and uncomfortable topics, now says that
as a teenager he stills comes to her with questions about
drugs. These are questions she would never have dared ask
her own parents. You should tell your children that they

can come to you with any problem, and stress the word *any*. Assure them that you won't pounce on them. Let them know that they should talk to you before putting themselves into scary or dangerous situations. But add that you understand that their curiosity and the power of temptation are strong, and that if they aren't able to talk to you before doing something dangerous, they should certainly talk to you immediately afterward. Point out that nothing they could do would cause you to stop loving them and that it's never too late for them to ask for your help. It's also a good idea to name adult friends, neighbors, or teachers to whom your children can turn if they have a problem they are afraid to tell you about.

• *New Move 10: If you're a recovering alcoholic or drug abuser, let your kids be part of your progress.* Admit to them that you made a mistake and that you once abused drugs or alcohol. Explain that you are getting help and show them how you've changed. Now that you are taking responsibility for your behavior, you should set limits and give them order in their lives, too. Most important, assure them that you love them, unconditionally, and begin to pay close attention to their needs and wants. As you listen closely to them, you may hear their true voices for the first time in your life together. Both you and they will reap the benefits.

• *New Move 11: Explain that it's okay to say no to friends and acquaintances who want them to do unsafe or unhealthy things.* It may not be drugs yet, but young school-age kids on their own for the first time can be tempted to do such things as ride their bikes in the road or take other risks. Encourage your children to love themselves and protect their bodies from harm. All your efforts to bolster your children's self-esteem will contribute to their natural sense of self-protection. There will be times when a child will worry that she will lose a friend if she doesn't agree to go along with something that's harmful or dangerous. You should tell her that her fear may have some basis to it, that at times such disagreements do cause rifts between friends. But explain as well that someone who would ask you to put yourself at risk is not much of a friend to lose.

10
Talking About Your Children in Front of Them

- "She is just like my sister—clumsy as an elephant."
- "This is my artistic son, and this is my smart one."
- "You're just like your father. Your temper is atrocious."
- "If she doesn't go back to school soon, I'm going to go nuts."

As children we heard our parents do it, and so as parents ourselves, we often make the same mistake. You say something to or about your child within his earshot. Though you intend it as an innocent remark, your child interprets it very differently. To him, it may sound like a judgment you have passed on him. And whether you realize it or not, you may be passing a lot of these judgments about your children in front of them.

Whether you say it to the child directly, or she hears you say it to others, what you say about a child communicates reams about what you think of her, and thereby contributes substantially to the child's own definition of herself.

The reason these parental evaluations take up such a prominent place in the child's self-image is that at the core of a child's identity is how he believes his parents view him. At times this can work to a child's advantage. A woman I know remembers her father always telling her what a tough kid she was. "She can handle anything," he'd brag to others. "You're tough," he'd tell her, "just like your old man." To this day, whenever things get rough, and she wonders if she'll get through some trying time, she recalls her father's characterization of her: "Dad always said I'm tough. I can do it!"

But even such positive evaluations of a child's capabilities can work against him. If you believe that your choice is to tough it out on your own or disappoint your parent, you may end up unable to ask for help when you really need it. It goes almost without saying that when parental evaluations are pointedly negative, the effects can be devastating. Tell a child he's clumsy often enough, and he may never try out for any athletic teams. Complain that he never does anything right, and he may begin to grow into a ne'er-do-well.

As parents, we sometimes forget that kids often take negative comments more seriously than we do. First, adults learn to make small talk, just to be sociable, and often fill this small talk with what they believe to be amusing but innocuous characterizations about others. Children hear these characterizations as well-thought-out ideas.

Second, adults learn to evaluate a criticism made of them in the context of all their strengths and weaknesses. But young kids frequently see things from an all-or-nothing point of view. You mention that his room is dirty and off-handedly call him a slob. You may mean it for that moment only, but he incorporates it into his sense of himself.

Even clearly positive expectations can cause problems. Within your child's earshot, you brag to Grandma about your child's participation in the gifted and talented program. You tell him that you think he's the smartest child in school. Now he feels that he must never make a mistake. He looks at other bright kids in his class and wonders what will happen if you learn about them—will you be disappointed in him? Or you tell your child of your fondest wishes for his future, that you hope he'll grow up to be a wonderful doctor like his father. But he secretly wants to be a teacher and now feels troubled that you won't like the profession he chooses.

To some extent, talking about your child in front of him can be a no-win proposition. Will your positive comments bring too much pressure to bear, or will a negative comment be taken too much to heart? And what parent hasn't blurted out something not meant for a child's ears, something the parent would do anything to take back?

On top of all this, some children may take what you say with a grain of salt, while others are devastated by the smallest negative comment. A lot has to do with a child's inborn temperament. You may try your best never to demand perfection, and still find yourself with a perfectionist on your hands. You may never utter the words "She's shy" and still have a shy child. And these children may be the ones with whom you'll have to be most careful. They came into life with some strong defining personality traits that may surprise you, and you have to be particularly cautious about what you say about these characteristics, so that you don't exacerbate the situation.

But even if these defining traits don't surprise you, you should always take into account your child's temperament when saying something about him that he will hear or

learn of. Think about it from his point of view. Ask yourself how he, given his personality, will likely be taking your
comments.

Parents' Expectations

The comments you make about and to your children contribute to their perceptions of what you want of them, so
you need to be careful not to trample on their own goals,
dreams, and most natural inclinations when you express
what you expect of them.

Too often, parents bring their own agenda to what they
say about their children. One mother I know, an inveterate
joiner, is always complaining to anyone who will listen that
her daughter never gets involved in after-school group activities. The child herself, who is much more a one-on-one
kind of person than her mother, is beginning to feel as
though there's something wrong with her, simply because
she's not like her mother.

Too many parents expect that the laws of heredity guarantee that their own children will be like themselves. Others
formulate an elevated vision of what their children will be
like as adults, and some even communicate to their children
that they owe it to their parents to try to reach this ideal.
Sometimes children do fulfill or even exceed the highest
expectations of their parents. But if they've done it only to
please their parents, there may be a high cost attached.

Ultimately, it's impossible to predict the precise impact
that your statements about your children will have on them.
Their understanding of what is being said of them may be
far removed from what you intended. You tell a cute story,
thinking it shows what a sweet child you have. But your
child may think you're mocking him. So it's a good idea to

try to imagine how your children will hear something you intend to say before you go ahead and say it.

If your child is not in the habit of openly volunteering how he feels about things, it may be wise to ask him occasionally for his reaction to what you've said about him to others. Some kids let you know in no uncertain terms when they feel you've embarrassed, pressured, or offended them; with others it has to be wheedled out of them.

The Child's-Eye View

From toddlerhood to school age, children grow increasingly aware of how their parents' words and actions reflect their parents' perception of them. But parents don't always realize just how much a child may be reading into the smallest item of verbal or even nonverbal communication.

Toddlers

Though toddlers are somewhat less able than older children to interpret the words used to address or describe them, they will pick up on your tone of voice, your body language, and your impatience. You may never express the thought that you're a little concerned about your toddler's slow progress in developing manual dexterity, but when you grab the shoe she's trying to put on out of her hands and shove it on her foot quickly, she gets the message. Of course, every parent has moments when time constraints almost force such reactions. But a toddler whose parents regularly show respect and admiration for her efforts at independence will really blossom. The same goes for her endless climbing up and down stairs or her interest in opening and closing a drawer a million times. When time and patience allow, applaud your toddler's efforts to gain mastery over simple tasks. Your positive response encourages her to feel good about herself and her abilities.

What may be even more difficult is to restrain yourself from roughly handing your toddler over to another adult after a long day of caring for this whirlwind. Again, your tone of voice will be felt by your toddler more than the actual words you say: "I can't get a thing done with him underfoot!"

Though obviously no parent can rise above these feelings of exasperation all the time, you should make an effort to keep them in check. Your toddler's sense of himself is developing at this age, and he depends on you to show through voice and action that you care deeply about him despite your feelings of exasperation.

Preschool-Age Children

A preschool-age child is more verbal and has a greater understanding of what you're saying about him. He's also become aware of social situations where an adult may be evaluating him. If an adult walks into a preschool classroom, for example, every child will begin to put on a show, because this is the age at which children start to care about what adults think of them, and each child assumes himself to be the center of attention. As a result of these new concerns about adult recognition, the preschooler is starting to be quite sensitive to what he hears you say about him to others. He may not always understand all the words, especially because parents often talk in code in front of children this age, but he may understand he's being talked about and dislike it.

Parents sometimes make the mistake of telling others about a preschooler's needs and wants—before the child has had a chance to speak up for himself. She may need a few seconds to respond to questions. If a parent is always rushing in to fill any silent moment, the child does not get a chance to gain mastery over her communication skills— indeed, she may learn that it does not pay to think before you speak. Your child may also be offended that you are presuming to know how she feels or what she wants to say to others.

Another factor that comes into play here is that a pre- schooler can be quite sensitive to your telling others about his strengths and weaknesses. He's already started to be- come aware that he isn't good at everything, and it frustrates him to hear you point that out. Besides, kids should never hear you make judgments about them because such re- marks can limit even further their own sense of what they can and can't do.

Preschoolers will also begin to feel embarrassed about stories you tell others about their babyish ways, such as having a security blanket or sucking a thumb. Your pre- schooler may now be even more sensitive to gestures of nonconfidence than when she was a toddler. You grab the orange juice away before she has a chance to try pouring it. Or you say impatiently, "Let me do it, I'll take care of it," as though you don't have any trust in her abilities. A preschooler may also be more sensitive than you realize about out-loud comparisons you make to his siblings, es- pecially older ones. In fact, all it may take to hit a sensitive nerve is encouraging him to do something an older sib- ling did at that age. One mother I know, whose older child learned his letters at a very young age, began talking about letters with her second child at that same young age. But he just wasn't that interested. "Gee," she said innocently, "Matthew loved doing his letters when he was your age!" To which her preschooler replied loudly: "Me not Matthew!"

Young School-Age Children

Your grade-school-age child will be most sensitive of all to the comments and remarks you make about him to others. As he comes out of the egocentricity of early childhood and becomes more social, his sensitivity about being criticized, and being spoken about, increases dramatically, because he's now very conscious of how others view him. In addition, he finds himself in many more situations where his abilities and talents are being tested. He's making friends and learning about social interactions on a regular basis. The pressure of school, the new challenges before him, and the standing he is achieving among his peers may make him more aware than ever before of what his parents think of him.

Because your child is old enough to be more articulate about her feelings but young enough to still be sharing many of those feelings with you, this is also an age when you may have a golden opportunity to find out what she really thinks of your statements about her. When one mother of a school-age child made the mistake of telling her son he was selfish, he followed her around for an hour defending himself by reciting all the ways in which he had proved himself to be an unselfish person.

Missteps Parents Make

We are all products of our past. And in many families talking about the children as though they weren't there, or talking to children in ways that unintentionally undermine

their sense of self, was often the order of the day. So it's
no wonder that many parents find themselves saying to
their children the same things they heard as kids. Here are
the most common missteps.

• *Labeling a child negatively.* Any negative label, regularly
applied, can become a self-fulfilling prophecy. Calling a
child a slob, a klutz, a troublemaker, or a goof-off, either
to her or in angry complaint to your spouse, relatives, or
friends, can almost guarantee that the child will come to
think of herself that way. This is especially true if you pre-
face your labels with "You're always such a . . ."

One mother I know says that there's a school-age boy in
her neighborhood whom she once praised for being kind
to her son. The boy is always courteous, well-behaved, and
polite whenever he bicycles by and will often stop to talk
for a few minutes. She found out recently, to her shock,
that he has been labeled a troublemaker by everyone from
his parents to his teachers. And he apparently obliges them
with behavior to fulfill their expectations. But she's never
seen a trace of it; remembering her praise of him, he tries
to live up to the image of the kind boy her words created.

• *Overpraising or bragging about your child.* Parents today
want to avoid the mistakes they feel their parents made. I
know one mother who can recall the two times in her entire
childhood when she was praised. She remembers the feeling of joy upon overhearing her mother whisper to a friend,
"She's as bright as a penny." But some parents can make
the mistake of overpraising or bragging about a child. I
remember one youngster I knew, whose parents overgen-
erously praised a poem he wrote. They talked about it for
days, made copies to send to friends and relatives, and even

mailed it to the local newspaper. The child never wrote another poem, apparently convinced he could never again meet the extraordinary standards implied by his parents' gushing enthusiasm.

Overpraising can also have a very different effect. Rather than suffer nervousness about his ability to live up to your expectations, he buys into it, hook, line, and sinker, and begins to believe he can do no wrong. But his inflated sense of his own talents may make his inevitable first failure a devastating experience.

Overpraising can also confuse a child, especially when he knows that he does not deserve the brass-band treatment you're giving him. He knows that there are other children as bright or talented as he is, and your too-expansive praise may cause him to begin discounting your judgment. Your opinion loses meaning when he knows he is not being evaluated accurately.

Bragging about your child to others can also devalue him as a person. He may come to feel that you love his achievements more than you love him. He may wonder if you'll still love him when he fails to exceed his last performance or if he does something wrong.

• *Talking about a child's problems or weaknesses as though she or he were not in the room.* Every parent has been tempted to do this. You're having a conversation with a friend or a relative about some problem your son is having. You're fretting and you really need to tell someone, but you forget that your child is probably fretting about it, too. Whether his teacher says he never pays attention, or he's still wetting the bed, you divulge some secret, and he suddenly sits bolt-upright. "Mom!" he remonstrates, before running from the room in tears.

You've exposed your child in a very painful way. We all deserve to have private matters kept private, and he may begin to feel panicked that he can't trust you to keep his secrets.

Furthermore, you must also understand that when you talk about a child as if you couldn't care less whether he hears you or not, you strip him of his sense of presence. A child's sense of self is enhanced by feeling that he has an impact on others, and when others seem unaware or unconcerned about his possible reaction to what is said, he begins to doubt that he is entitled to respect. In time, he may come to believe that his feelings truly don't matter.

• *Comparing siblings in front of them.* Nothing can be more enraging to a child of almost any age than hearing "Your brother would never do such a thing" or "Why can't you be more like your sister?" Sometimes parents mean well and try to find nice things to say about each sibling but still wind up in trouble. For example, the child who repeatedly hears that he's artistic, while his older brother is the intellectual one, may believe he can't achieve academically and therefore shouldn't bother trying.

Any way you compare children, you're bound to exacerbate siblings' already heightened feelings of competition, as well as the sense of rivalry between them for your high regard. Your innocent question, "Aren't you going to try a musical instrument at school?" or "Will you go out for the baseball team?" may communicate to your child that you'd like him to walk in his older sibling's footsteps.

You should be especially careful not to make comparisons while both siblings are in the room. The one suffering in the comparison will feel doubly humiliated that his or her sibling was allowed to hear it. And the one being praised may feel a mixture of glee and guilt for getting accolades at a sibling's expense. I know a woman who is still hiding good news about her successful career from her siblings because they have always teased her, sometimes not good-naturedly, about being the fair-haired child their parents always praised.

• *Telling cute stories about or laughing at a child.* Many parents I know remember being laughed at as children. Or they remember being the butt of some family joke that was repeated over and over again at every holiday occasion. Young children miss the fine points of jokes or stories but remember the feeling of humiliation. You can't expect children to accept jokes at their expense in a good-natured way, or to understand that adults do not intend to mock children when they make jokes at their expense. Saying to a child, "I'm not laughing at you; it's just that you're so cute," doesn't comfort the child or assure him that you're really on his side.

• *Ranting about the difficulties of parenting.* "She's driving me crazy, I can't wait for school to start," said an exasperated mother recently, while her daughter stared up at her. All of us joke good-humoredly about the challenges of parenting. But if you're doing it in front of your child, you may cause her to feel that she really is a burden that you'd rather not have around. You certainly never want your child to hear you wish her away.

• *Telling kids that they've inherited your own or your spouse's traits.* "You are just like your father. Your temper is atrocious." Especially in families where the parents are fighting or are divorced, it's hard to avoid blurting out comments such as these. For recently divorced parents, the children may serve as haunting reminders of the person who has brought so much grief to the other. But you have to be careful that your children don't bear the brunt of anger that's not really intended for them. Sometimes even a child's physical characteristics—the shape of a nose or the type of hair—can become the focus of an angry comment if it reminds one parent of the former spouse.

A child should not be expected to change traits that in and of themselves aren't negative, just because they remind you of your former spouse. What if your ex was a nonstop talker and your child is, too? His chatter may remind you of your former spouse, but it's also your child's way of being himself, and you do your child a disservice if you press him to squelch his natural personality just to spare you reminders of an unhappy relationship with his other parent.

• *Discussing a child's punishment with your spouse in front of the child.* It's a form of public humiliation to rattle off a litany of your child's transgressions and then discuss possible punishments while she is in the room. The child is essentially listening to her fate being decided. Parents should discuss between themselves the course of action to be followed, and then sit down with the child, in private, and out of earshot of siblings or other household members, to communicate a punishment or to request a change in behavior. A discussion of possible punishments that includes input and suggestions from the child does have some merit—she's more likely to respect a decision she helped you reach—but even here a prior discussion between parents would be helpful. Certainly make sure others butt out.

• *Suggesting to your children that you'll live vicariously through their achievements.* Children shouldn't feel burdened by your unrealized dreams. Don't put yourself down and then tell them that they won't make the same mistakes you did: "I was never very good, but you'll be terrific." They may wind up feeling guilty when they do achieve what you did not. Or they may begin to fear that in the end, no matter how hard they try to avoid your mistakes, they will fail, just as you did.

The most important point on this subject may be that your living vicariously through them doesn't respect their individuality. They simply may not want to try to achieve in those areas where you failed, or do the things you never had a chance to do. There is nothing so sad as an adult who in middle life recognizes that he has achieved his parents' dream for him, but at the expense of his own.

New Moves

The underlying theme of each of the new moves described below is that you ought to treat your child with respect and attempt to see things from her point of view. In doing this, you convey to her that she is worthy of your regard for her as her own person. When you start with these givens, you'll find it much easier not to talk about your children in front of them in a way that will hurt or trouble them.

• *New Move 1: Give your child affirmations.* Affirmations are statements that tell your children you have confidence in them. They declare to a child that you believe in him. One man remembered that his father once said to him, "Son, you have a good head on your shoulders. You're going to amount to something." Over the years, his father's words often gave him confidence when he most needed it. Affirmations don't suggest that you expect perfection from your child. They simply tell him that you think he's capable and competent just because of who he is.

• *New Move 2: Tell your children that you accept them as valuable and unique members of your family.* Each of your children should feel that he or she is a significant member of your family group. Tell each one, "I'm really glad you're part of this family." Make clear that your acceptance isn't based on performance in school or at the piano, but that you appreciate the child's unique personality traits, talents, and abilities—even if they aren't the same as yours or those of his or her siblings. In essence, you're telling each of your children that you don't wish that child were someone else.

• *New Move 3: Check with your kids before divulging secrets about them.* There will be occasions—in front of a doctor or a teacher, for example—when you and your child will need to go into something she may find embarrassing. Prepare her and ask her whether she'd like to bring the topic up or if she feels awkward and prefers that you bring it up. If neither seems acceptable, take the doctor or teacher aside and ask her or him to bring it up. Or in certain cases that don't involve health or safety issues, respect your child's wishes and just keep quiet.

• *New Move 4: Praise children appropriately.* The key to reasonable praise is to do it only when it is deserved and appropriate. A woman I know always resented her parents lavishing praise on her schoolwork. She was really a rather mediocre student and an average achiever. But her parents were teachers and they believed that schoolwork was the area to praise. A better course would have been to praise her true talents, which rested in caring tenderly for animals and being a good listener. Discerning and praising a child's true gifts, even if they don't fit in with your view of success, is the key to helping kids feel good about themselves.

• *New Move 5: Criticize children with sensitivity.* When you must express disappointment because of something a child has done, be critical without being heavy-handed. When your child is calling a younger brother or sister names, for example, you might say, "I know he gets on your nerves when you have to spend a lot of time with him." This opening statement lets your child know that you are acknowledging her feelings and her problems in dealing with the younger sibling. But then you should proceed with your criticism: "Even though you feel that way, you have to know that calling him names hurts his feelings." Then let her know that you believe she's capable of better behavior: "I know you can be more sensitive because I've seen you do it." Finally, help her work out a solution to the problem: "If you feel that you can't stand him anymore, come and tell me before you start calling him names. I'll help you."

• *New Move 6: Rather than labeling kids, analyze the behavior behind the label.* Sit down with a "troublemaker" and ask him for his version of the story. Maybe the fight he got into at school that day wasn't his fault. Your attempts to learn what happened from your child's point of view helps him feel that you still respect him and aren't 100 percent against him. In the end, you may come to believe that he needs to be punished, but he'll know that you gave him a chance to have his say and did not accept the label someone else put on him.

Behaviors at home can be approached the same way. Instead of calling a child a slob, express your anger at the mess he made. If you roll up your sleeves and work with him as he cleans it up, he won't feel that you're attacking him, and your participation in solving the problem tells him you're still on his side.

11
Always in Front
of the Children

I've attempted to provide strategies you can use during those many occasions when you're not quite sure how to talk about sensitive or uncomfortable topics in front of your children. If you feel as though you've already gone through situations where you didn't say just the right things, be comforted by this: it is rare that parents are not presented with second opportunities to raise issues they handled badly the first time around.

A child's ego grows, in part, through attempts to surmount adversity, solve demanding problems, and tolerate unpleasant feelings—all natural by-products of living. If you go to extraordinary lengths to shield children from all of life's adverse moments, you rob them of the vital experiences they require to grow on. Children need to learn that while life offers much that is pleasant and enjoyable, it also offers much that is not.

They need to know, for example, that arguing is usually

unpleasant but may be a constructive and even at times necessary part of the process by which people resolve differences. When you and your spouse argue, you should talk to your children about it. They should be made to understand that arguments need not prophesy doom. And when you're angry, they can be told that, too, provided they are simultaneously shown that anger need not always be destructive. What is of major importance is that children see the resolution of your arguments, so they that may learn that people who love each other work out their conflicts rather than allow a dispute to continue to cause pain to both parties.

While preserving parental privacy is important, children should always see expressions of warmth and love between their parents. You are, after all, the role models for their own later relationships. They should also know that sex is a significant part of life and that you are there and approachable when they have questions on the subject.

If your marriage is in crisis or you have divorced, there are still valuable lessons to be learned by your children. You can teach them that you will be honest about painful circumstances that affect them. They should be assured that they are part of the process, that both parents recognize the pain they are suffering, and that both are concerned about their future welfare. Information offered children must assure them that they were not the cause of the difficulties between you and your spouse and should lower their anxiety about their own lives in the changed family circumstances.

When it comes to serious illnesses and death, your children need to know that these, too, are part of life. They need to see that there are times when even their parents feel very sad. They need to know that you respect them sufficiently not to exclude them from urgent family matters. They need to be allowed to mourn along with the rest of the family. And, finally, they need to know that they can speak about death and at times be irreverent about the subject if this helps them cope better.

If financial problems come up in your family, children need to see their parents cope with this kind of crisis, plan strategies for dealing with it, and take steps to confront the future realistically, but with hope and resolution. Children who learn that families pull together during times of strain are well served for their future lives. On a more practical level, all but the youngest children get a valuable beginner course in coping with money problems as they watch their parents struggle with financial problems through refinancing loans and other steps designed to add order to the family resources. To avoid having austerity budgeting totally deprive your children of the fun their childhood owes them, creative efforts should be made to find inexpensive recreational activities the family can share on weekends and holidays.

If a substance-abuse problem exists, children should be told the truth, so that they do not doubt their judgment about harsh realities they observe. Children also need to learn that there are positive ways to cope with stress, so that they won't feel that smoking, drinking, or drug use are appropriate responses to emotional problems. Likewise, they need to be shown that drugs and alcohol aren't integral to happy times; that exercise, hobbies, and other forms of relaxation, performed individually or as a family, can be far more pleasurable and rewarding.

Always in Front of the Children

Whether it's an argument, a divorce, a death in the family, a child who's stumbled into his parents' room while they're making love, living with a substance-abusing family member, or becoming aware of any one or more of the countless everyday matters that all families regularly face, such moments demand clear-thinking parents. While each of the preceding chapters has outlined specific strategies to use in particular situations, here are some general guiding principles that will help you in all of them:

• *Always overestimate rather than underestimate how much your children have noticed and heard.* Even your most intense efforts to keep the truth from them will not prevent them from having a pretty good guess at it. And if you overestimate, you won't run the risk of leaving your children to wrestle alone with something they've seen or heard.

• *Always assume that your children will misunderstand what they have heard and seen.* Children, with their limited experience, will not perceive situations the same way you do, and unless you exercise extreme care, you run the risk of having them misinterpret your words. You must take the time to break down what you say into language they can comprehend.

• *Always choose your words carefully.* Keep in mind the ages of your children and how capable they are of understanding complex, adult-centered events. A good rule of thumb is always to ask them first for their thoughts on what they believe happened. Then correct any misconceptions or fill in the gaps where they display only partial understanding. Of course, you don't want to overload them with detail that they don't have the intellectual or emotional maturity to grasp.

• *Always assure your children that you are in control.* Even though you may be upset by events, make sure the kids know that you are taking steps to deal with whatever problems the family is facing. You might invite suggestions, but children need to know that you don't expect them to shoulder responsibilities that are too heavy or in other ways inappropriate for them. You are the adult, and it is your job to find solutions.

• *Always corroborate your children's accurate perceptions.* If they say they saw a relative who was drunk, and they are right, confirm that they were correct. If your child witnessed an argument between you and your spouse, admit that you were having a disagreement. Otherwise, children begin to doubt their own ability to evaluate the events and situations they have observed.

• *Always be honest about your feelings.* Children are entitled to know when you feel sad, or angry, or frustrated.

• *Always permit your child to express his feelings, whether you like them or not.* Children should never be humiliated, shamed, or berated because their thoughts or feelings seem immature or poorly founded. Accept that they feel the way they do, and take it from there.

• *Always take seriously a child's point of view.* Even though a child's thoughts and concerns may seem trivial from an adult perspective, they are important and meaningful to the child. They also may contain clues to the fears or concerns your child has that you will need to address.

• *Always admit it when you've made a mistake.* It's okay to make mistakes. In fact, it's inevitable. No matter how hard we try, at some point we are bound to say or do something we later wish we had not. It's important for parents to admit when they have done something inappropriate and say, "I'm sorry." Children should know that you understand the value of an apology and respect them enough to offer one when you have offended them.

By honoring a child's right to knowledge, you buttress his sense that he is a respected member of the family. Subterfuge, outright lying, and other forms of fraud are not only fruitless but can provide a blueprint for a child's own later temptations to evade the truth or even deceive himself in difficult situations. Furthermore, children who are deprived of essential information about their family life when their intuition and perception tell them that something is amiss develop clusters of cloudy, vague, and amorphous memories. They grow up feeling as though a blanket had been thrown over chunks of their life. The gaps in their knowledge leave them feeling perplexed and confused. As adults, they have a difficult time knowing what was imagined and what was real.

If you try your best to keep your children properly informed, they will appreciate your efforts and be strengthened by them. And you, in turn, will be rewarded by having children with an accurate perception of reality and a strong sense of self.

Index